COPIKAZE

A Crucible to Manage Mission Impossible

THOMAS RIZZO

DEDICATION

This book is dedicated to everyone who chose to love me as I painfully learned the messages contained herein and exposed my vulnerabilities.

Some colleagues, some friends, some foes, and all those in between contributed in some regard.

My wife, my children, and my intimate family (yes some without formal blood relation) are owed a debt of my gratitude too great to fill. You are the fuel to my fire and the source of my most compassionate admiration. I love you more than you'll ever know.

CONTENTS

INTRODUCTION

The path of a career in law enforcement encompasses light, darkness, tranquility, terror, risk, and reward, all intertwined, with each component having odd codependency of one another. This path is unique and offers a front-row seat to the most incredible show on Earth; the wonders of life. The navigation of this path and its traveler would equally enjoy a tremendous benefit if a guide were to be composed, not just for prospect or retrospect, but for reference as a turn-by-turn directory.

This manual of sorts would afford its reader much greater chances of an enjoyable ride from the onset of the career journey, not only as a means of avoiding the potential hazards of the adventure as they present themselves. In the ideal form, this crucible of knowledge would be carved by an officer who has served honorably in the field, garnered with scars and citations alike, surrounded with the earned respect of peers, who can recite the hymns of glorious battle cries, sing the songs of the fraternal joys, and share in the shedding of tears for those lost but not forgotten.

The imagery of the infantile officer standing beside the grizzly veteran is worth more than a thousand words as to if the images portrayed could only speak to tell us how each viewed the world from the start of their trek to their near completion. In relevance to the profession, nature is more intelligent than people think, as are the effects it can cause. As one of mother nature's many profound mysteries, some species' baptism has been intriguingly captured on film, including some dangerous feats.

A crew of researchers, recently focused on filming a documentary, set out, and with cameras rolling, hoped to memorialize their hypotheses. The crew would amazingly observe barnacle goslings hobble their first awkward steps from the safety of their nests and, without hesitation, intentionally tumbled downward on a cliff face in their native Greenland, as they could not yet take flight. Despite each gosling watching a sibling's failed attempt, some fatal, they noted one constant control; the next would follow, in a rhythmic cadence, regardless of the definitive plummet lying ahead.

As the chronicles of wartime history eerily hold painstaking memories, I find a peculiar correlation between the choice of becoming a law enforcement officer and that of the notorious Japanese "Kamikaze" pilots of the World War II era. In the most simplistic manner of describing this sadistic combat tactic, these suicidal soldiers would use their aircraft as pilot-guided missiles to strike enemy vessels, despite their dreadful outcome of the deliberate flight maneuver. Incapable of reconsideration, with full disclosure of what was expected of them, individuals willingly accepted the mission as part of what they saw to be a noble cause.

An unimaginable sense of madness must have been a prerequisite for such enlistment. Yet, interestingly, that same sense of madness has become a similar statement of cause and assignment in the debate arena of who would possibly want to become a police officer considering the advent of modern times.

Most would concur that the law enforcement profession comprises a much more sophisticated trajectory course with prescribed safeguards for its prospective officers than would be that of a gosling in Greenland or the determined Kamikaze pilots in WWII. Yet, as each year passes, despite self-proclaimed advancements, members of law enforcement only experience increases in intentional self-inflicted harms and a blind following of "that's the way we've always done it." I've yet to encounter someone tasked with the tremendous responsibility of recruiting, retaining, and developing police personnel who would intentionally pave this particular crash course; however, I have encountered consistent resistance when I earnestly provide suggestions to alter it. Despite factual basis and scientific evidence that some internal industry trends are counterintuitive to wellness, we press on clinging to the adage, "if it ain't broke, you can't fix it."

The times of denial have come and gone. Agreement and consensus are readily available when I present the argument, especially to colleagues, that we, ourselves, have created some scenarios for our fellow officers, which are ripe with impending doom; however, when seeking participative collaboration as a resolution strategy, I haven't found that same fortune of agreeableness. Allow this literature to serve as a "how-to" manual of sorts, not just how to avoid certain horrific consequences of poor choices, but so much more significantly, how I hope that you will learn to follow a pathway to enjoy a fruitful career balanced with a fulfilled and wholesome personal life.

For those readers who are not sworn or prospective law enforcement professionals (retired or formerly employed), whether you are intimately related, intrigued, or combative to the profession as a whole, allow this book to serve as some insight. This book explores the personal journey, the pitfalls, hurdles, the wins and losses, the smiles and cries. This book does not answer the cliches, the shallow-ended questions like Boston cream or a bear claw? Ticket quotas? Whether or not bonuses are proffered to an officer for arresting a particular person? By no means is this meant to solicit or garner agreement on all aspects of the profession by non-police persons, but to offer, at the very least, a glimpse of sporadic understanding, without expectation of a solidified support. Understanding in any fragment of the term would certainly benefit both sides. My genuine hope is that this will help heal, not hurt, advance, not arrogate, uplift, not upend, and enlighten, not endanger our collaborative chances at a better future for this profession and its stakeholders' personal lives to thrive, not just survive.

CHAPTER 1

Mission Statement

My career started in New Jersey, while the dust had not even finished its solemn descent from the catastrophic events of September 11, 2001. I considered my comprehension of the law enforcement profession's mission to be without void, a patriotic semblance based on the cliché of protecting and serving.

Armed with the sixth sense to observe the unobservable and predict the unpredictable, as I blasted through the exit gate of my academy graduation, I felt a firm grasp that I possessed all of the necessary fabric to weave a security blanket of a successful career.

As a plumber is equipped to handle the routine and not-so routine plumbing emergencies, I would be that surety of law and order, internalizing my organization's mission statement into a living document of deliberate action.

A mission statement, loosely defined, is an organization's statement of existence or purpose.

Some notorious examples:

- **NYPD** – "The mission of the New York City Police Department is to enhance the quality of life in New York City by working in partnership with the community to enforce the law, preserve peace, protect the people, reduce fear, and maintain order."
- **LAPD** – "It is the mission of the Los Angeles Police Department to safeguard the lives and property of the people we serve, to reduce the incidence and fear of crime, and to enhance public safety while working with the diverse communities to improve their quality of life. Our mandate is to do so with honor and integrity while at all times conducting ourselves with the highest ethical standards to maintain public confidence."
- **SEATTLE PD** – "The mission of the Seattle Police Department is to prevent crime, enforce the law, and support quality public safety by delivering respectful, professional, and dependable police services."

With absolutely no intention of casting disrespect toward the fine men/women of these departments, I'd venture to guess those same men/women feel everything but in harmony with the sentiments held within their mission statements compared to the actions encouraged of them in the field.

Thankfully, since the evolution of current-day social

networking vehicles, it has become entirely plausible to obtain background information about any department's inner workings before seeking employment with that same department. One does not have to rely upon the department's mission statement as a sole marketing tool to find out the truths of operational expectations once a formal assignment has already begun.

Misalignment of mission statements and the expected behavioral norms within an agency is a recipe for specific disastrous outcomes.

The creation of moral tennis matches in terms of "what we say" in contrast to "what we do" fosters interpersonal conflict. We cannot continue to act surprised as to when outrageous outcomes result from the propaganda culture we have helped to create. The profession has created a false sense of commitment in the obligatory formulation and advertisement of these statements of purpose.

As I am writing this book, each of the agencies used for illustrative purposes above have been infected by outside influences to allow a tolerance of disobedience, not just contradiction of the message, but utter hypocrisy as to what the mission states compares to what the mission actually is.

While the preferred current manner of mission statement composition may be to gather a group of words meant to numb any potential critic's senses, the reality of field operations can denigrate the reputation sought.

Although I intended to work for a large-scale law enforcement agency, comprised of an abundance of opportunities for my career to flourish, I found that life's timings and my appetite to set onward could not be suppressed.

THIS YOUNG AND INNOCENT EAGERNESS WOULD SERVE AS THE FIRST OF MANY LESSONS TO COME:

Not everything goes to plan and fits in a neatly packaged box.

The inability to accept this and forced feed oneself strict adherence to rigid expectations will consistently lead to easily avoidable disappointment. Learn to roll with the punches and realize that you gain something from not always getting what you want; experience.

After finding a way to expedite the completion of my undergraduate bachelor's degree sooner than some (three years), not because of intelligence, but because of initiative (I will share that lesson later), I found myself in my first career conundrum. Do I sit in the state of a psychological waiting room for nearly a year for an announcement of the next hiring process for the department which satisfies my taste palate? Or, do I punch in no matter the origin of the patch I wear, as long as I am wearing a shield?

The answer was so readily apparent, and twenty years later, I can say, without reluctance, that I don't regret a thing. Although not listed in my personally-prescribed blueprints, I found myself being sworn in by a municipal department based in a small jurisdiction, comprised of only thirty-five officers, who all seemed to have some tie of familial bond with the township. I vividly remember the deafening silence when asked, during my interview, what I knew of the town. I struggled, blurting out that I knew where to find the police department, and that was about it. Thankfully they had a sense of humor. To their credit, the Chief and administrative panel decided to take a risk and snap a tradition of legacy hiring ingrained with nepotistic trends by choosing me, an outsider, for which I'll be forever grateful.

I'm convinced that the vast range of emotions individuals experience as they embark on the journey of a career in law enforcement cannot be truly comprehended by those who have not walked that path. I do not provide that statement with cause to be presumptuous or outright elite, but instead to call to common senses in that some things are not capable of being fully comprehended by those who have not intimately experienced them, and that is perfectly acceptable. Being transparent to an extent, open to conversation as to the how's and why's are preferred over a state of inertia; however, juvenile anticipation of having the civilian sector gain a full understanding of the profession after being exposed to a single training initiative or demonstration is utterly irresponsible. I can personally sit at the bedside for an entire shift with an emergency room physician in one of the most reputed hospitals but would still not be able to proclaim that I know much about their life candidly.

Snapshots? Yes. Panoramic views? No.

I believe our current training academy environments need a dire update (more to follow on that). But, upon my graduation and start of my training, I felt equipped with all I needed to get the vehicle in motion, or at least I believed I had a complete toolbox.

No, that does not serve as a hint of a newly-hired

officer instinctual obligation to empty the shelves of a local law enforcement outfitter.

A LESSON TO THE TRAINERS OUT THERE:

We train dogs, we should "develop" people.

Tactics, procedures, and tasks can be taught to anyone. Teaching the personal side of the career and the immeasurable value of how to treat and interact with people from all walks of life should be paramount and how the profession impacts an officer's health. The overemphasis placed upon trainers to impart the contents of volumes of procedural books in the time it usually takes to read one article is a failed endeavor. A training shift in gaining an appreciation for human behavior and the appropriate reaction would benefit the trainee exponentially compared to the traditional means.

Despite being assigned field training officers with extremely distinct backgrounds and work ethics, my insatiable curiosity to learn all facets of the profession, both on/off-duty, persisted. I had the sense of innocence not to be deflated by the fact that I represented a vital "checkbox" for an insider Sergeant candidate, who was one of my trainers.

The order was handed down to temporarily reassign a career Detective and Chief's favorite to serve as a field training officer. Despite having no prior experience in training and an extended sabbatical from relatable patrol duties, his role in my successful completion of the field training program (introductory training curriculum provided to newly academy-graduated officers) would provide the means to be "justifiably" promoted in the upcoming selection process.

We can all relate to the pressure felt by being the central figure of the "You better not screw this up for me" scenario.

ANOTHER LESSON:

It's not you I swear, it's me.

Innocence is not your enemy. Not everything is personal. Sometimes you're innocently incorporated into objectives beyond your control. Embrace these situations by having eagle eyes, kangaroo ears, and a mouse mouth.

I immediately gravitated toward a particular training officer, who displayed a concentrated interest in criminal apprehension, with a unique blend of informal department respect. While it was apparent he was not privileged to eat plump grapes at the Chief's pristine table, I felt emulating his behavior would be more suitable for my career aspirations.

Although frustrating at times then and to this day, I've found this particular behavior pattern to be paramount to genuine happiness, wherein I present:

A CRITICAL LESSON:

Define what really matters to you.

For true fulfillment, follow what fills your gut, not your pockets. Your gut will feed the rest of your days well beyond the depth of any pocket.

I don't purport to be a sensationalist or fraudulent shaman. We cannot address life's financial obligations with hugs and sunshine. Trust me; I get it. You can find the evidence of my claim among your own set of contacts and social networks. Think of someone who has sold their soul now devoid of any true calling or has all their pockets can hold. Examine this thought to yourself: Does he/she seem genuinely fulfilled? Living in a perpetual state of acorn gathering creates an unfillable gut. If you feel like something of an area you've visited is foreign as to what you represent, avoid occupying the real estate there. Although the four walls may be present, the rooms within the structure are empty.

I allowed my gut to dictate where I would focus my energy, and I was off to the races. Again, I did not fall victim to all of the latest and greatest gadgets to allegedly assist me in my endeavors. Still, I internalized what I understood as the mission at hand. My head was on a swivel, and if would-be offenders crossed my path, I had an obligation to identify and apprehend them. If the need arose to assist someone, who summoned that assistance, I'd naturally respond with the utmost level of customer service. However, I understood my role (sworn as my oath) as the plumber example set forth previously to be readily capable in applying my unique set of skills; crime fighter.

Early afternoon hours on a weekday, as autumn patiently awaited its formal entrance to New Jersey, during the latter part of my twelve-hour shift, an unimpressive sedan passed my location on the only state highway the jurisdiction had within its bounds. The champagne color was quite common at the time. With the absence of any apparent equipment violations, advertising its invite for a citation, I'd categorize this vehicle as an everyday mover. As any truthful officer should admit, sometimes it's simply a matter of right place, right time, opportunistic passing of glances. I observed two individuals occupying the sedan.

Both individuals had a reaction to my presence with the classic expression; bulging eyes followed by hide and seek within the passenger compartment from what they thought would be my view of them. They were not happy to come across my marked patrol vehicle and almost immediately turned into a residential neighborhood. As I followed behind the sedan, I observed the driver throw the remnants of a cigarette out of the window, leading to the constitutional justification for a motor vehicle stop. After the motor vehicle stop, using my basic sense of sight/smell/hearing, I discovered both individuals possessed personal use marijuana and cocaine.

Did this stop and subsequent arrest set any relevant state records? Of course not, and I'd venture a guess that it would be the furthest from any such proclamation. The interesting perspective of the stop was that evidence of a neighboring jurisdiction's recent armed robbery was also located within the vehicle, and both subjects were previously identified as viable suspects therein. A simple littering violation turned motor vehicle stop, turned narcotics arrest, turned violent criminal apprehension. My ego soared.

Feeling a sense of adrenaline compared to seismic activity within my veins as I returned to the station, as a rookie officer on his way to great things, I was immediately brought back to Earth's mere mortal platform of reality. I was summoned to the Chief's office for what would be a recognition ceremony. As I entered, I noticed a short stack of garage sale-style signs strategically placed adjacent to his desk, on the floor, while he sat silent. I was sure that my face became filled with a reddish tint as a concoction of emotions began their physiological effects.

It was well established that the Chief despised the unauthorized placement of such advertisements on utility poles. It was a department-wide responsibility of patrol officers to ensure strict compliance during their tours within their designated areas. Most will read that statement and recite a quip to themselves. I've tattooed the memory of how I tried like hell to preserve what I felt to be pride in what I had accomplished, via my stop/arrest, compared to the disgrace I was about to be reminded of for neglecting my utility pole preservation duty. With still no utterance of audible sound, he made the slightest hand gesture toward the signs, which I accepted as "get these the hell out of my office," and so I did precisely that.

Despite my best attempts to not personally harp on this incident and the plethora of inputs surrounding it, I soon realized that I failed. This realization presented itself in various forms, including undeniable manifestations such as cynical behavior, commiseration callings, misguided tantrums toward my then-girlfriend (now loving wife), and most of all, a dented sense of spirit.

The sound of a deflating balloon sums up the sounds of my sighs for days after that, with not a single colleague offering me an alternative view.

I didn't get it. What was the mission? The Chief, who lived in the same proximity as the department and stop, was more upset that I failed to tear down the garage sale signs than he was pleased with the fact that I apprehended two felons on the same roads his family traversed daily.

What did they expect of me? I was unclear, and it led to confusion, and the confusion led to criticism. I shielded stress with sarcasm. Even though I observed these same tolls previously paid for by my training officer, who I was sure that emulation of his tactics was the path for me, I failed to embrace this event with any sense of grace.

Knowing it was incumbent upon me to steer my ship and go back to the drawing board, I turned inward toward self-reflection.

Considering I was at the embryonic stage of my career, not willing to settle for years of work drudgery, I created a few priceless points of reference that have served me well ever since.

———

THE LESSON FROM THIS EXPERIENCE:

Run your mission.

Formulate your mission while being mindful and proficient at the mission of the organization. Realize your mission statement is a living thing within your soul and being. Your organization's mission statement is a standard of generic advertisement meant to appease the calls of what we "think" is expected of us and what sounds appealing to anyone who should so desire to read it. The organization's mission statement sets the "tone" for the agency, but the individual officer's mission statement should be the "song" chosen by him/her. Be aware of the organization's needs, grow your mission statement to add nutrients to that same organization, not poison. Suppose your mission statement is at the complete opposite end of the spectrum of the agency's mission statement. In that case, you must alter your direction of travel. If not, you'll undoubtedly end up at destination misery.

About three years after being hired, I was the first officer in the department's history to transfer to another agency. I do not assign my decision to transfer as a resolution to the climate as mentioned earlier or any combination of negative feelings. I accepted an opportunity with the larger agency of which my original intentions were to join since childhood. The "me" now would tell the "me" then that my previous Chief was not a bad man with the evil predisposition of thwarting my initiative. Life itself has taught me not to prescribe my personal beliefs as the belief or preference of others. That is ignorance at its finest.

As much as his leadership style and sense of prioritization perplexed my overall senses, I had to accept the fact that both are "his" and that they don't necessarily have to be "mine." His preferences and coveted aspects of the daily activities were no secret. It was well within my intellectual and behavioral control span to tolerate this and be prepared for the expected outcome if I was to act in a contrary manner, as in the scenario I referenced. It became apparent that I must acknowledge my actions and the full disclosure of the probable outcome as I operated outside of the parameters.

In the case cited herein, I knowingly procrastinated in tending to the signage placed on the poles in my sector to conduct my interdiction staging. I chose to do that. Me. When the powers that be show any noticeable disappointment or make any disparaging remarks about my chosen actions, I cannot construct a society called "The world against Tom township." My mission is my mission, and the organization's mission existed before the tabulation of mine.

As an industry, we should provide our personnel missions that do not foster misconceptions or preconceived convictions to a false narrative. Far too many officers become disenchanted when these epiphany occasions occur, such as mine. This disenchantment can be avoided if we were to be candid with what we honestly expect from our officers compared to what sounds marketable when hung on the walls of our halls. Upon announcement of my impending transfer, claims were made that I had the potential to lead the agency in the future.

DESPITE PROMISES OF PREDICTED PROSPERITY, I LEARNED THIS FINAL LESSON ABOUT THE MISSION:

Control your own destiny.

If something is misaligned between you and the organization, contribute to the alignment process instead of focusing on the discord, projection of blame, and lack of parallels. After formulating your mission statement, allow for flexibility and adaptation. Commit to your objectives and create a symbolic ballistic barrier capable of shielding those objectives from others' insecurity, bitterness, and doubt. Have no fear of failure. Have a fear of never committing to what you truly want to be.

CHAPTER 2

A Look in the Mirror

C hances are, and with relative ease, you can recall the definitive or descriptive slogan for the police identity. I am sure the first thought you may have is "Protect & Serve". No? Maybe it was another option from the myriad of sensual catchphrases referring to the effervescent sheepdog's artistic depictions who protect the vulnerable from the ferocious wolves of society; there is certainly no shortage of inputs. A more genuine question to ponder would be to debate who we are and what we represent. I'm not one to deny the true or sorely needed existence of society's sheepdogs; however, let's say that "a sheepdog" is not necessarily the primary object of comparison my mind would choose when confronted with the instinctual first impression of an officer. Where does the mind travel when prompted like an internet search engine for an officer's suggested image?

I've consistently recommended a priceless piece of equipment, which no officer can afford to go without; a simple, compact mirror. Although we can use this gem for tactical situations and grooming inspections, that's not my intention here. The periodical use of the mirror should be something each officer uses to present an intense stare meant to serve as an examination of oneself. Effectiveness will be achieved not by only asking, "Who am I?", but more comprehensively internalizing the thought process of "Who have I become?", "Who do I want to be?", and last but certainly not least, "Who can I never be?". Many theorists have suggested the undeniable strength of self-introspect in identifying areas in need of growth or attention. While our vision tends to routinely be free of obstruction, when looking at external objects, mirrors of our reflection tend to get fogged over by the clouds of denial.

"Who am I?" has a laundry list of potential responses depending on a variety of the ingredients used for the personal creation of the being. Consider an examination of law enforcement officers' stereotypical norms or behavior modalities from across the United States. Despite extreme distinctions when officers from all four corners of the country are asked about their tendencies and routine habits, certain personality staples or values become readily apparent as majority-based. So, who am I? I am you. You are me. We are most. Most family-oriented individuals are selfless. Most are family oriented. Most are empathetic and compassionate. Most are loyal. Most are good.

Various psychological assessments are deemed reliable measuring devices for officers' mental acuity, actually relying upon the "most people" standard in terms of a balancing act. Questions and scenarios are presented, which then compare the individual officer's response to how "most people" would react with the same impetus. While I fully agree with the importance of connectivity between officer candidates/officers as they progress/officers as they near retirement with that of "most/normal people", I wholeheartedly object to the intolerance spewed at the industry when these same preferred personality profiles are observed in non-flattering situations. Society's one-way-styled street only wants officers to act like "most people" so that would-be psychopaths do not become authorized to enforce the law; Agreed. However, if an officer on the typical Tuesday was to display the slightest grimace of frustration at what "most people" would as well, a definitive demeanor complaint is undoubtedly forthcoming. Secret reveal for the non-officer reader; what pisses you off, pisses us off too. We try like hell to numb and dumb our senses, but our hearts/minds/blood-flow cannot be thwarted when we work a shift despite remarkable technological advances.

The general description pertaining to the "I" within the question can figuratively be provided with a sense of ease. The next layer of "What have I become?", incorporates difficulty if the response intends to be a factual self-analysis on behalf of the respondent. Just as in any other scientific experiment, evaluation, or estimation, the intended outcome is accuracy. Accuracy within this paradigm is based upon candor, no matter if the response is complimentary or insulting. Ego preservation tactics will only serve as an impediment to the fundamentals of the initiative. Regardless of service time, officers will undergo a metamorphosis as their career progresses. The "become" can be unintended, unforeseen, and unpredictable.

Recognition of the "become" is paramount to harness

the positive outcomes and cleanse the negative effectively. Despite what some antagonists may proffer as expert opinion, there is much more to the "become" than a damaged and irreparable soul infested with Pac-Man style bites. Most of us "become" equipped with a new sense of awareness for the many facets of life's happenings. An innate sense of appreciation occurs (various ways to allow this to blossom will be covered later). What else do we "become" though?

Stop for a moment and let your conscience adequately digest this question while not allowing your noble defense mechanisms to deny the truth.

Unfortunately, it is all too often that the officers themselves are the last to recognize the "become", as the loved ones are those with the emotional scars from there.

You see, they know full well what we've become yet are often fearful of our response should they ever venture out on the precarious limb of such a hint to us.

So, "What have I become?"; cynical, pessimistic, critical, non-trusting, suspicious, selfish, jealous, depressed. This is not an all-inclusive list, nor is it meant to indicate that I feel downtrodden. It does, however, represent many traits which the profession caused to metastasize within my makeup.

Maybe I've had these traits all along, maybe not, but I can identify that they were bolstered by my years as an officer without any reservation. Internal and external variables within our profession's dynamics cause these outcomes to be nearly inevitable yet rarely focused upon by training mechanisms to combat or appropriately govern them.

From our academy training to our working environments filled with our negative contributions, external pressures, and constant judgment on how closely we meet unattainable standards, the recipe to bake this "become" cake is complete.

THE LESSON ON "BECOME":

Recognition of Change.

Recognize what you've become not by focusing on the present but on what changed. Something was the primary catalyst for the change. The first step to eradicating a disease is to identify it and then attack its likely causes. There's nothing to be ashamed of if your "become" is not an ideal model. It is, however, a shame to recognize the undesirable "become" and to do absolutely nothing about changing it. Progress and advancement do not occur overnight, nor does "becoming" something we wish we hadn't. Incremental adjustments to the "become" are the most effective in keeping these inevitable transformations modest. Commitment to a disciplined cognizance of these changes is well worth the compounded interest it'll bear in the sense of wellness, longevity, and prosperity.

If tasked, most could easily imagine and compose a vivid description of an individual they wished to emulate or imitate. As a child's mind can almost instantly transpose their face onto the body of a superhero, the newly hired officer should always strive to have a target of admiration. The "Who do I want to be?" segment of this experiment certainly can vary as it depends on what the officer personally covets the most. The selection of the individual worthy of this emulation is the simplistic stage of this process. However, the rationalization as to the choice of the officer requires insight and introspection. As the adage states, "If you hang out in a barbershop long enough, you'll end up getting a haircut." A few years will pass for many of us, and we find ourselves suddenly stuck in the mud. Any creative thought process or dreams of grandeur have already been embarrassingly shot down by our peers, which we've allowed.

I recall being a young, wide-eyed Patrol Officer, so intrigued by interdiction that I submitted a request to attend a national training symposium. As an avid learner and student of the game, to be amongst the industry's best was something of a daydream. I was soon sobered by others' inability to foster dreams, only to face a cynical response from my direct supervisor based on a tone of overwhelming sarcasm. I was referred to agencies working at the border if I was interested in such things and that I should focus on the "everyday things" instead.

We, unfortunately, allow ourselves and our goals to become prisoners of others' insecurity, negative energy, and ill-will. The result of this tends to be that officers aspire "to be" a figure of mediocrity. I'm a personal fan of Lynyrd Skynyrd's "Simple Man" as it so eloquently tampers expectations..." forget your lust for the rich man's gold, All that you need is in your soul." The point of this mediocrity allegation is that there is an overabundance of officers who don't correctly assign themselves a target model to inspire them to foster further progress. The outcome of this is that the individual officer starts to falsely believe they've maxed out in terms of potential. Successful, driven, and secure people surround themselves with those of similar mindsets. Notice there is no mention of clout, privilege, or position, but a positive mindset is a common theme. When we dig a little deeper, we often discover these individuals to be uncommon, accomplished, and wealthy, but not due to some form of undeserved gratuity. These individuals have earned their status primarily due to their mindsets and those they've properly chosen to emulate. This mindset lends the individual the ability to essentially reverse-engineer success. I'll put it this way; If I wanted to enhance a particular skill, I'd seek out the best in the game and intensely study them, instead of missing such opportunities only to be replaced with weak excuses or ignorant signs of disbelief incited by my insecurity. These determined individuals' interactions are smothered in curiosity and fearless conversations, not sarcastic remarks carefully chosen to hide unhealthy envy. Those plagued with the inability to do so will find themselves offering statements of unsubstantiated criticisms or consistent rationales as to why the targets of their negative sentiment should not enjoy their relative accomplishment.

THE LESSON HERE:

The carrot, the egg, and the coffee bean.

Find someone worthy of your admiration and emulation. Have the courage to seek out how they got to where they are and

whether or not you are willing to sacrifice the same as they did
to get where you want to be. For most, success is not a
coincidence. Choose your idol carefully and deliberately, so he/she
serves you as a source of nutrition, not poison. For the best choice
of who to become, utilize the message found within the parable
of the carrot, egg, and coffee bean as to how each allows the
outside influences (boiling water) to affect what they become.
When placed in boiling water, the carrot soon softens and
implodes from its lack of ability to hold its true form. The egg
soon will harden and ward off any attempts of the water to re-
penetrate it. However, the coffee bean takes the water and
reverses the course while transforming the water, not itself, into
coffee.

In the depths of our collective minds or the halls of our
coffee-time conversations, we have all shared commen-
taries about the people we swore we would never become:
The political patron, the ambassador of disingenuous
gestures, the dunce, the pincushion, or the incorrigible.
I've often found it ironic that the question of "Who can I
never be?" in law enforcement can be answered to the
point of causing a raucous if in a group setting. It strikingly
resembles a group of adolescents posed with a challenge to
provide the most slang terminology for genital body parts.
On the personal side of the "never becomes," some will
affirm these claims about addiction, abuses, or even infidelity. Having a gauge of what you will "never become" also
provides insight into what you are or what you intend to
become.

Our subconscious self tells us what to steer clear from
in many ways; however, we often find ourselves unable to

avoid repeating the "never become" in terms of past actions. Did you ever find yourself complacent in repeating the exact behavior of someone you swore never to repeat, simply because it was the path of least resistance? I consistently implore officers to savor the taste of the ill-behavior by those deserving of your "never be." If their behavior nearly made you vomit, then why would others feel different if you behaved the same way? The point is, the establishment of extreme "do not enter" zones for behavior simultaneously sets a personal scale for the ideal behavior for you to abide by.

THERE IS A VALUABLE LESSON TO BE TAKEN FROM THIS:

"I've not failed, I've just found 10,000 ways that won't work!"
-Thomas Edison (On Discovering Electricity)

Study and examine someone you swear never to become. By closely observing this undesirable personal behavior, you can also observe the effect it has on others. Consider the information gained to be a free education of how NOT to treat others. Diving further into the analysis, earnestly try to determine the causation of the actor's ill behavior. Not only may this afford you tolerance for someone, maybe undeserving before analysis, but it will also offer you another preemptive warning of what causal factors to avoid at all costs so that you don't unnecessarily expose yourself.

If some of our current leaders theorized these elementary questions, perhaps some of the dilemmas we face could have been mitigated by common sense. The lack of individualized presentation or thought about these questions presents several issues. Leaders are all too often not confronted with a candid sense of others' perception due to fear of reprisal, fear of contradiction, fear of consequence, or in the worst-case scenario, fear of retaliation.

The result is the creation of the leader's single dimension vision, which has a myriad of external influences, most commonly lacking the influences of those who matter most; operational-level officers.

As a gauge of personal sentiment, leaders tend to rely on an obligatory salute offered by those commanded to do so, instead of the deliberate failure by that same "saluter" to even hold the door as a common courtesy, which is the more accurate gauge of what is being felt, compared to what is forcibly being shown.

The importance of this point cannot be understated. When leaders lose their identities to the position's intricacies and statutory authorities, the organization's identity becomes lost.

Depending on the leader's stature, in terms of stage size and notoriety, the potential impact that the applicable loss of his/her identity could be felt on the stakeholders; the officers could be catastrophic.

A LESSON TO TAKE:

Identity crisis averted.

The only means to realizing you're losing yourself is to first have a genuine grasp of who you really are to begin with. Embracing who you are opens the doors to what you can offer to others.

By no way am I suggesting that personal changes are the demon of a police career. Lord knows I've been a chameleon of sorts as the development and maturation of emotional intelligence can certainly add tolerance to once-rigid positions or personal stances. Changes of views or positions can be fluid, natural, and welcomed, just as changes in physical appearance can be (loss of weight, different physical goals, hairstyles, etc.). As long as the skeleton and core remain, as they will if built on the sturdiest of foundations, superficial or ideological changes can occur without such irreparable damage as we've seen of late. Once considered staples of the law enforcement profession are now given perplexed looks by the officers they command due to severe shifts away from what we all felt sacred. When the leader lets the winds or the tides steer the ship instead of their sturdy grip, the organization's soul is swept along just as the ship is unguided.

I've been blessed to interact with law enforcement personnel throughout the country, expanding as distant from my home state of New Jersey to New Zealand and Australia. Through these intriguing interactions, I never miss the opportunity to pose a question, which I've

commonly used as a classroom poll; Do you prefer to lead
or follow? Overwhelmingly, whether the respondent is an
individual from a foreign land or a local classroom of
student officers, the reply is to "lead" because that is what
most would think is the "appropriate" response. However,
when explained the numerous examples of how subordinate
our law enforcement culture naturally is, the respondent
will realize the lack of accuracy in the initial response and
genuinely state they prefer to follow, with the caveat being
to follow the "right" person. The most straightforward
manner to find the "right" person is by finding those who
have found themselves. I do not intend to present this
point as a negative attribute of our profession in that it is
subordinate in nature. Subordination is an integral part of
the description pertaining to the "Who are we?" debate. We
are subordinate to a system of laws, rules, regulations,
governance, authority clauses, leadership hierarchies, and
the unavoidable political machine. I do not personally
subscribe to a belief that the current system should be over-
thrown or feel it's prudent to arrange rallies for a revolt. I
do, however, teach others the practice of being intelligently
insubordinate. To some, the two words may seem to contradict each other, but the pairing is meant to be symbolic of a
creative thought process. Instead of simply carrying on our
serviceable years with blind subordination to what any fool
could easily recognize as moronic policy initiatives, counterintuitive to both reality and wellness, I recommend seeking
clarification. Seeking clarification should never be confused
with what has been informally assigned to Generation Y
regarding constant questioning for the purpose of action.

Upon being confronted with lunatic policy implementation, I highly recommend that you seek clarification while combining your inquiry with an alternative resolution. Not even the most astute of leaders enjoy the thousand-question series without having a dependable source of resolution strategies provided simultaneously as he/she receives the questions. By only ever offering what appears as a contradiction to orders, shock the conscience and provide a way to accomplish the objective "better," while being mindful that the definition of "better" can undoubtedly be in the eye of the beholder. When enacted properly, even when offerings of improvised methods are denied, the pattern is established for the officer offering such as an innovator within the organization over that of just a squeaky wheel.

In terms of identity, the climate of modern-day policing has been somewhat a result of the perfect storm with the use of 2020 as an illustrative year. The aforementioned perfect storm has been brewing long before the turn of the calendar or a single impetus. When our industry allows leaders to present falsehoods of identity, gaggles of individuals subscribe to a platform lacking the foundation as mentioned above.

As it crumbles, which has been repeatedly observed, so does the morale within. The commonality now for current officers to begin phrases with, "I never thought we'd be doing..." is staggering and reaches far beyond those who thought that the implementation of Miranda Warnings would be the end to proactive policing as we knew it. No, this is different. If we, as a culture, do not constructively rebuild a foundation of who "we" are and covet the honor therein, we risk losing one of our fondest traditions; solidarity.

THE FINAL LESSON ON OUR IDENTITY:

Find your authenticity.

No matter what the abundance of propaganda may tell us, know yourself. Know who you are and what you represent. Do not depend on what the propaganda suggests you are and what you allegedly represent by mere associative epitaphs. Be flexible and adaptable as to your mental/behavioral subscriptions. These are the keys to longevity, not just career longevity, but life longevity. When the crystallization of the true self occurs, embraced with wellness, wholeness, and alignment, greatness becomes possible. Only placing fingers in the dam as each small crevice presents itself will never provide a solidified barrier from water leaks. Find a way to genuinely establish your defined dam.

CHAPTER 3

Jekyll & Hyde The devil we know

Officer Jones' alarm chimes, it's 6:30 am, and the news anchor's solemn tone suggests an unfolding headline. He's grown accustomed to keeping his television on as a source of white noise as a means of helping him sleep. But this time, he awakens to the news of another senseless act committed by society's darkness, and he immediately assumes the predictable sensory overload, which has become part of an unintended routine.

The officer ambushed on routine patrol, the innocent child left victim to a turf war, the repeat offender who played the judicial system like a revolving door game. These examples are listed herein as illustrations, but I welcome you to insert your substitutions.

Make no mistake; whatever substitute is chosen, they are equally incendiary to the civil servant's soul and the cause of psychological warfare. It may be the preferred outward appearance of a "Dr. Jekyll" in most cases of a uniformed officer, which we hope to encounter when the reality is that "Mr. Hyde" is alive and well within the inner workings of that same officer.

Dr. Jekyll is the unblemished billboard of poise and professionalism, happy to help, and eager to participate in the multitude of philanthropic outreach programs. Mr. Hyde is that bitter taste left behind, yet ever so prevalent despite the attempts to wash it from the memory of our palate. He is left behind by every experience or subterfuge that we assign to humanity, despite what our field time impresses upon us.

I've been an outspoken critic of the age-old expectation that police officers should represent robotic depictions of human beings in terms of preconceived notions they may have possessed before the days of pinning a shield to their shirts. Despite the catchphrases or sensitivity-driven statements that proudly display just how "woke" we should purport to be, a confrontation is unavoidable if the soul conflicts with the expected expression.

Do not allow your tactically-driven minds to dive into the traditional sense of the term "confrontation" instantly. The "confrontation" can rear its ugly head and materialize itself in several ways. The notorious "Officer Hothead" is the most simplistic fashion, but I choose to focus on the much more prevalent yet under-studied models. The taboo, but ever so prevalent, feeling of utter disgust that infringes on the officer's mentality when they directly witness an innocent person suffer a tragedy, only to see a remorseless villain who goes on to thrive.

These internal struggles remain kept within the vaults of officer's minds as the fear of public consequences surmount any measurable chance of presenting candor.

Imagine the reaction if an officer suggested a particular perpetrator repulsed every fiber of their soul due to the horrendous nature of the offense committed. The response to hearing the fabled stories of the fleeing felon who shoots with his off-hand, backward, in the opposite direction, while running, penetrating the officer's center mass; now the officer, who's trained for years suffers a weapon malfunction while standing rigid in the proper shooting position, yet is rendered defenseless. Murphy's law never seems to miss an opportunity for the "good guys".

I am well aware that these feelings contradict the outward appearance we must present. Still, the study, acknowledgment, and revelation that this contradiction finds its home base is the strategic purpose for its inclusion in this book. To mention a few "bases"; stress, heart disease, stroke, relationship fails, depression, loss of concern for oneself, substance abuse, domestic violence, loss of spirit, and disenchantment.

While it is much more colorful to share viral videos of the eruption of this internal confrontation in the forms of officers shouting honest feelings toward the most "deserving" of individuals (I can recall one of a Connecticut State Trooper that had me in warped tears of laughter), the more silent manifestation of this confrontation has been the source of our downfalls.

This internal struggle with what the reality of our patrolled societies represents, compared to what is advertised, has caused more physical and mental deterioration than we will ever care to admit. This constant ringing in our heads of what we "really feel" in stark contrast to how we "must act" would cause any sane person to question the same level of sanity.

I can candidly acknowledge feeling somewhat distraught at a recent community service-based initiative, where officers provided toys and meals to families who submitted requests for assistance. Instead of feeling overcome with joy as a gleeful participant in a venture to "help those in need," I instead allowed Mr. Hyde to rear his ugly head as I examined the "needy" to be holding the latest model cellular telephones.

At the same time, the other hands carefully guarded a freshly-lit cigarette from a $10.00 pack. Perhaps, I wouldn't have knowingly invited Mr. Hyde to my brain's party, if during normal times, these needy parents reinforced or displayed signs of support for law enforcement instead of simply accepting tangible benefits offered by the same.

As I stood there, amongst other officers, offering a holiday greeting, I could not deny the existence of these thoughts, which was everything but a greeting.

To discuss or even admit this, however, is taboo outside the walls of our departments. William Butler Yeats wrote a famous poem entitled, "An Irish Airman Foresees His Death." In the poem, he writes, "Those that I fight I do not hate, Those that I guard I do not love." This perfect imperfection of the duties we perform serves as the pride and detriment of the profession simultaneously.

THE LESSON HERE:

The Cost of Candor.

I've come to learn the power of open and honest discussion, despite having inherent risks. At one specific career crossroad, I was the recipient of a young male's offering of a middle finger as I passed a strip mall in a marked patrol unit. I remember approaching him as his cohorts fled the area and questioned him as to why. I gave no orders, never shouted any commands, and gave no threats of any consequence. I just asked why. To my surprise, he offered a quick whisper that he has officers in his family, and his group was threatening him if he did not give me the finger. Did I love his lack of courage to resist something he did not stand for? No. But, I was reinforced that this was not just another hater by simply asking the question.

As a magician hones his craft of creating illusions, the utilization of such terminology as "preconceived notions" creates an illusion when presented to a group of students, no matter the setting. The mind almost definitively syncs to a reference of bigotry.

This synchronization is nearly absolute if the student body primarily consists of law enforcement, which directly results from the institutionalized manner of how we (law enforcement) process rational thoughts.

Officer Jones, as an illustration, was raised as a devout Christian, who can rapidly recite biblical passages when prompted, and values the family unit above all else. This background was very well known and provided to his department before joining the ranks. Officer Jones enjoys sharing his beliefs and openly invites his coworkers to Sunday services, where he is an ordained minister.

Yet, when Officer Jones responds to a residence numerous times in a week for a domestic disturbance, where the intoxicated father figure beat his wife and abused his children, his supervisor is annoyed at his lack of overt courtesy toward the suspect.

With no policy violations noted, no infraction to un- fract, no regulation to regulate, we lose the ability to realize that we've come to expect Officer Jones' blind enforcement of the law to be devoid of any sense of influ- ence of who he is or who he was, long before arriving at that house.

This expectation provides a bounty of a feast to the appetite of Mr. Hyde. This expectation of numbness also serves to cater to alleged offenders' demands and prioritize their appeasement tolerance over the officers' wellbeing. This catering has been created and allowed to thrive based upon our fear of what "people" may think, despite what the facts themselves represent.

I am no proponent of unprofessional demeanor toward the general public; however, I am opposed to blanket policy standards without any room for deviation depending on the circumstances. Requiring Officer Jones to interact with such persons while yielding a bitter beer face smile is fraudulent and antagonistic to our instincts. Yet again, 'feel good food' for Mr. Hyde's appetite.

Officer Jones and those like him are readily capable of professionally performing their duties, accompanied by their personal backgrounds; however, when they feel abandoned by the same moral code required of them for the appointment, the conflict thrives.

When Officer Jones sees the recurring theme of the offender's feelings being considered above the victim or the responding officers, this conflict is exacerbated.

Officer Jones will be privy to secretive reassurance from his peers that his feelings toward the offender are justified and shared by the masses. But in no way, shape, or form can this consensus of sentiment be shared beyond the confines of his locker room walls, as our leadership has so vehemently warned.

THE LESSON HERE:

It's business. It's not personal.

There are various aspects of this profession that would undoubtedly qualify for reassurance of the individual officer's reactions. Am I normal feeling this way? Seeking out reassurance is not a sign of weakness. You should hold your source of reassurance in the highest regard. Do not mistake simple complicity of thoughts and feelings as reassurance.

Be prepared to be offered differences of opinion and constructive criticism. You can often find different perspectives outside of your profession. I was taught this lesson by the owner of a small-scale pizzeria about not taking things personally. That is how you grow out of the unprosperous fraternity of misery loves company.

Several officers of various ranks and roles have asked

me if I think it "really matters" if our leadership is vocal about the challenges staring them in the face. Without any shade of reluctance, I can state that it absolutely matters and how a prominent display of support can be the most effective form of contraception to Mr. Hyde's chances of successful breeding within a given department.

I've made it a habit to contact officers from departments where I've observed someone in a leadership capacity be outspoken by proudly employing common sense rhetoric on a particular issue worthy of media controversy.

To no personal surprise, the officers from these respective departments are fully aware that the impact of their leader(s) may not even be deemed worthy of three-seconds of news coverage from the same outlets covering the controversial issue itself, but is priceless to them and reassuring to the psyche, above all else. A sense of invigoration occurs when officers realize that their administration "has their back." I do not intend to invoke ignorance by the placement of such a slogan and suggest creating a system with lackluster oversight.

The support reference relates to the fact that officers working in environments where administrations routinely propel them into the center of the prosecution coliseum, despite their rigid adherence to law and policy, are the same that suffer from the highest rates of officer depression, fatigue, and suicide.

THE LESSON HERE:

Give the gift that keeps on giving.

To be equipped with the confidence that they are being led by those who easily identify right from wrong and are certainly not afraid to state such is a gift to an officer. The gift of not having their livelihoods discarded like a widely-distributed coupon circular remains sacred to officers. This gift helps keep Mr. Hyde in check.

In the current policing environment, we fail to acknowledge that it is physically impossible for officers not to be affected by the daily occurrences they are informed of, nevermind the hazards they are exposed to on the job. With the advent of modern avenues of information sharing, at a moment's notice, Officer Jones can have his day completely altered when his smile turns to a frown, and his laughter turns to sobs. All this because of another sobering report of "something" that happened "somewhere" to "someone" who didn't deserve it. To effectuate the robotic reactions society has requested, which some administrations have prescribed, free from personal emotion, our officers would need to be raised in the most remote of wilderness preserves without access to any outside influence. This robotic manner sounds plausible to some, that is, until the need for discretion can benefit the same individual who feels robotics, with pre-programmed enforcement algorithms, should not apply to them. Automation in a field nearly overwhelmed by human-to-human interactions is not only impossible but an impediment to the service element. While free from attitude tone, automated messaging systems are also free from personally serving the caller. These pundits and fans of such systems are often those same individuals who will attest to have a 20/20 vision of a policing issue from hundreds of miles away. Any person, from any profession, would be boldly-faced lying if they suggested that the contributions of their non-work life did not directly correlate to their performance in their related work field.

LESSON:

The little voice upon my shoulder which softly whispers to my ears.

Personal emotions define and shape us as human beings. Overwhelmingly, these emotions are positive, uplifting, sentimental, empathetic and conducive to good intentions. Be aware of how much influence your emotions have on your actions in the field compared to the training you've received. Creating a harmonious partnership between your emotions and your training is critical. This harmony and balance are more easily achieved when one works in an environment known to support its stakeholders.

Some media platforms can serve as a fantastic asset to a law enforcement agency. The immediate dissemination of vital information, advertisement of initiatives, community notifications, etc., has propelled police departments' reach into uncharted territories. Mr. Hyde enjoys nothing more than a disingenuous post or viral message about department dealings. As the conveyor of the department message is watched by many, while most with intimate knowledge of the message itself make jerking motions with their hands/arms, the conflict of the statement and the reality of the situation erupts once again.

This vicious cycle is experienced repeatedly, yet we still surprise ourselves when the consequences surface. As Officer Jones finished witnessing the recent expose of a particular segment about his community by colleagues and supervisors alike, he is then told to respond to an event within that same community and fake a smile for the cameras, even though his presence at the event is not wanted, nor welcomed, nor genuine on his behalf. Instead of facilitating an honest discussion about why the officers feel the way they do compared to why that particular segment of the community feels the way they do, we allow the optics to prevail, so long as the picture looks good.

Superficial goal achieved, while Mr. Hyde is chuckling along the way. I have personally engaged civilians in a discussion about this very same dichotomy. I've been provided with a consensus of their reaction in that many of these depictions seem to be contrived and not genuine. Trust me, "they" get it, just like "we" do. While the majority of residents within our communities would welcome more open and unguarded communication opportunities, on the part of officers, these initiatives are often avoided like the plague. Some administrations have selective hearing and fail to hear these same residents as they do/have pledged understanding to our profession and are the ones to openly state, "they have a job to do", in terms of the police and policing. Any officer who has arrested a legitimate offender can attest to that exact quote being relayed by the same offender, who has now been apprehended. Is this to say that all criminal offenders are the most avid fans of the police? Of course not. The point is that we have created an atmosphere, due to our own manufacturing, in which we've created the script that all persons are incapable of understanding our role.

THE LESSON HERE:

Did you even catch a single word I actually said?

At times, senior law enforcement executives are so bitterly focused on "hearing" the needs of the communities they serve that they fail to "listen" to what those same communities adhere to and know. Active listening to what a person or people are saying is significantly different than simply recognizing audible tones that exit someone's mouth.

Why will Mr. Hyde seem to prevail inevitably? Transformational leadership can serve as the aptest gatekeeper for preserving the balance between the Jekyll and Hyde syndrome. If leaders know that Culture A prevails·within the four walls of the agency and certainly within the four walls of the officers' homes, yet expects the officers to display Culture B when they wear a uniform, something will inevitably fail. From avoidable and understandable demeanor complaints to the extremes of excessive uses of force, depression, or suicide, the system can be ripe for this interpersonal conflict. At the basic level, sincere commitment to recruitment initiatives is vital to gain representative stakeholders representing the culture they are committed to serving.

A close friend works as a deputy in a mid-size jurisdiction in central Texas. He was utterly floored when I questioned his community's level of interest and intensity bestowed to local high school football (literally businesses closed early on game nights). Imagine, for a moment, if I was to become Deputy Rizzo at this department and stop the assistant coach of the home team for a minor violation on his way to the game, for which he may now be late. Suppose the leadership failed to gauge my appreciation for the sport before my appointment while fully knowing that it is held in a religious state of reverence by the department's established members. In that case, they cannot be shocked when that coach complains of my innate ignorance. By no means am I opposed to diversity within the organization. Diversity in terms of backgrounds can create the most awesome forces, just as long as diversity does not subvert the community thread. Diversity should be considered as a means to enhance the reach of the agency, not detract. For the purposes of diversification, in the reference provided above, hiring Deputy Rizzo, a first of his kind for the department, who feels sports are overrated, within an agency sworn to uphold the high school football season above all else, we haven't achieved diversity. Instead, we've achieved avoidable animosity from all sides. This basic model can be used to plug and play however you see fit, as it is not

based upon advanced physics, no matter how hard we try
to pretend it is.

THE LESSON:

If something doesn't feel right, it probably isn't.

*Make your choices of employment worth it in terms of wellness
and personal/professional balance. Do not knowingly enter the
snake pit, only to act surprised when a snake lunges at you.
Alignment of what you represent and what your prospective
agency represents is key to avoiding the venom of Mr. Hyde. In
the interest of reciprocity, it would also be totally unfair to the
intended customers (community) if a civil servant is incapable of
understanding the customer's values. Alignment is not something
to be taken lightly on the part of the employee or the employer.*

Another tactic to contemplate in terms of this
balancing act would be something I've found to be life-
changing. Place the handheld electronics down for a
moment and have a face-to-face conversation with
someone who has absolutely nothing to do with law
enforcement. You may need to drink a shot of antacid, but
trust me, it'll be worth it.

Whether on the first or fiftieth attempt, you will find
that you are not expected to do/think/be the image you
and we have allowed to be created. The creation of this
image is the nucleus of the Jekyll/Hyde syndrome and
provides us with a level of unnecessary stress teeming with
anxiety. Ordinary, everyday people get it.

How many times have you encountered someone who says, "I don't know how you do what you do?" or something to the like. When we shield what we think and the internal person of who we are, Mr. Hyde lies in wait for the opportunity to strike. This career path can enlighten certain beliefs your Mr. Hyde may have had all along and foster them into a newfound understanding based on incredible positivity, not reinforced angst. I can proudly say that I've learned aspects about life, culture, and the world itself, through the experiences of being a police officer that has expanded my abilities exponentially, not restricted it.

I love seeing the reaction when I turn the table and present people with an intimate view of a situation from an officer's experience. With a careful and deliberate collaboration of my law enforcement experience blended with the human side of me as Tom Rizzo, rather than Officer Rizzo, I find growth opportunities. I don't expect our interaction to end with a permanent connection – rather a moment of understanding. This "moment" may never be shared, may never be admitted, but every time you do such a thing, Mr. Hyde has his strength decreased, and you will find that we are not so distantly apart from the civilian world.

FINAL LESSON:

Hello darkness, my old friend.

Becoming a police officer does not automatically require you to forget your likes, dislikes, preferences, and disgusts. Your Mr. Hyde is no different than many others. Allowing your Mr. Hyde to dictate your actions in the field is what needs to be curtailed. Engaging in a tug of war to deny its existence or the struggle to ensure that it never surfaces in your professional capacity has and always will have a breaking point. This frustration tolerance is different for everyone. Some can bear it, while others cannot. Recognize that you are not perfect, and the expectation of being such or being without sin is unrealistic, and it is irresponsible in ensuring wellness. Dr. Jekyll cannot be on-duty 24/7, and invariably Mr. Hyde will punch in at some point. Whether you shake his hand or slap it away is up to you. Turn your Mr. Hyde into something constructive and have open conversations about its existence.

CHAPTER 4

It is what it is

Ah, yes. The exhilarating feeling of having a stuffed schedule that affords millimeters of flexibility while making a necessary doctor's appointment is something I dread, almost as much as the physical visit itself. I'm not too fond of doctor's offices, the waiting rooms, the angst of vulnerability, the bad news, the white coats, the needles, and that sanitized smell. The signs say to be here within fifteen minutes of your appointment time—almost a cruel joke for the receptionist's pleasure.

After thirty minutes of waiting, I told the receptionist, "hey, I'm still on this side of the office." Her facial expression was one I can only attribute to a silent display of disgust and conscience shock. She replied to me by saying, "The Doctor is doing his best. It is what it is. Return to your seat and wait to be called."

I was fifteen minutes early. I had been waiting 30 minutes, plus some. I had still not seen the physician, and anxiety was now soaring through my mind and body, as I now fully expect to be late for my following scheduled obligation.

As I embraced my last particle of patience, I approached the front desk around the forty-five-minute mark. I kindly asked for an estimate of when the doctor would see me, as I recalled my appointment time, plus fifteen-minute pre-appointment arrival was an hour prior. I realized that this appointment and my chance of receiving decent results would now be doomed as my blood pressure was sure to set a record.

What would make the scenario mentioned above acceptable? What is the length of wait-time tolerance or deviation? I am not unique, nor is my experience here. Many have experienced a similar scenario, yet we've all swallowed the philosophy, which the receptionist stated so eloquently, that "it is what it is."

There is no genuine feeling of guilt or sorrow, given they have completely wasted your time. I get it, it is simply a part of doing a necessary business, and all have come to know that while eating it. Despite every online review of this particular location, highlighting frustration about this, the industry has a Teflon coating to any serious alteration, and the flock of patients will continue through the door, all while knowing what awaits them.

As the summer was ending, I decided to take my children to a local amusement park for a last hoorah, before the rigors of school set in. My daughter instantly races to a rollercoaster, with me following behind.

As I approached the park attendant, I noticed she was measured by the "height-pole," to which she met the standard, albeit by a fraction of an inch. To both of our dismay, the attendant, with a smug expression, says, "Maybe next year," as he explains that her forehead must reach the mark, not the "top" of her head. The confusion on my face was about as hidden as my daughter's anger, as any parent of an eight-year-old can imagine.

Understanding that height restrictions are based upon safety standards, we exited the ride, and I did my very best to explain this to my daughter at the level of a child's comprehension. I caught myself repeating the attendant's words, "Rules are rules," while watching other children be allowed entry, who measured identically to my daughter. It was unfair, inequitable, far from cool, unapologetic, but another prime example of "it is what it is." I was learning such a valuable lesson but did not have a true appreciation for the spirit of the message.

By using only these two examples, let's compare both scenarios to modern-day policing. If the police officer made an appointment to meet with someone and he/she followed your appointment scheduling to the finest detail, only to wait more than an hour, what would be the outcome if the response, to their well-posed question as to status, was, "it is what it is." Suppose the police officer was to stop a motorist for driving 26 m.p.h. in a 25 M.P.H. zone.

The officer issues a citation with a smug expression without any dialogue because hey, speeding is speeding. What would the outcome be if, upon receipt, the motorist looks at you with confusion, only to hear, "Now put your car in drive and follow the posted limits."

I carefully present this scenario as I'm sure there is some anomaly officer or situation out there that resembles this insanity. If you are or know of that officer, ponder this. Your unwelcomed approach to policing can have an effect or collateral damage that exceeds far beyond the bounds of your jurisdiction and scars the entire industry.

The law enforcement culture has created a semblance of apology first, no matter the surrounding circumstances, contributing factors, or facts themselves. From north, south, east to west, citizens (that means us too) encounter ridiculous treatment void of any humanity or appreciation every day, while that treatment is beyond worthy of the issuance of an apology.

The glaring difference between these industries where such treatment is commonplace (medical facilities, food establishments, entertainment venues, vacation markets, etc.) and law enforcement is that if they are confronted with a "wrong", they either rapidly apologize or offer excuses, then expeditiously move on never to revisit the issue.

THEY'VE LEARNED THE VALUABLE LESSON:

Am I eternally stained?

Harping on your shortcomings only welcomes further criticism, input, and attention on those shortcomings. Is acknowledging wrongdoing, a fault, a flaw commendable? Absolutely. Carve this on your forehead with a dull blade for eternity? Absolutely not.

On the other hand, law enforcement has habitually

apologized for doing what is required of them, with most apology-based incidents initiated by a perpetrator or violator. This initiation or active participation in a negative outcome, on behalf of the violator, is rarely given equal precedence to the officers' actions. I would never suggest that law enforcement is without flaw or never in need of the issuance of an apology. Still, the current climate of apologetic instinct has only hurt our industry. Apologies for the ultimate outcomes (death of someone, even if constitutionally justified) are appropriate, warranted, and recommended. I only wish this same empathetic approach to civilians was to be extended to officers. We've made it a routine to safeguard the judicial standard of "innocent until proven guilty" for everyone, except for our officers.

One of the many general rules to follow if the goal is to increase harmony at social gatherings would be to avoid conversation about politics and religion. Visualize the last holiday dinner when either was at the forefront of the conversation, and I bet the jolly was siphoned from the room within minutes.

With that in mind, while using the utmost sensitivity and caution, I will present some valuable lessons to be learned from both platforms regarding how we can benefit from their approaches to various controversies surrounding them. The only method I choose to analyze is their relevant approach to engaging their adversaries or antagonists, not their stances or positions.

Lest we paint with a broad brush, ponder, for a moment, the last controversial issue presented to either a politician or a church leader. Make this reflection personal in that it should relate to someone you identify with, being that you share a similar system of beliefs. Whether it's a prominent leader in the political party you prescribe to or a notable figure within the hierarchy of your religion of choice, reflect on an occurrence where they had to "face the music."

I was raised in a Roman Catholic background. While admittedly being far from devout, I must admit that I admired some aspects of the negative connotations about how they were dealt with. I was floored as a young adult when I witnessed parishioners' reaction when a diocese priest was relocated after being identified as a child sex predator. As quickly as it was brought to the surface for all to know, the situation and even the utterance of his name were just as expeditiously buried within the archives. While the repulsive behavior was addressed as being a stark contrasting representation of church norms, it was more of a "there's nothing more to see here" event and let us move on.

As a matter of fact, the common catchphrase used was based on the sentiment of not passing judgment on the entire priesthood based upon one's actions. Consensus was reached. Were the individual priest's actions disparaging to the parish and the faith? Yes, but the fundamentals of the priesthood were still held sacred, and the faith-based following agreed not to cast a wide net of reprisal. Sound familiar?

A more vulnerable target for this experiment could easily be that of a politician, where hard evidence of negative behavior, inexcusable mistakes, "mis-spokes," etc., all readily exist. Yet, despite the viewer of such evidence having perfect vision and hearing abilities, that politician manages to thrive as if all have been infected with selective amnesia.

Their thriving depends on just how proficient they are in placing the blanket over their heads so that the monster cannot see or get them, as we all once did as children in our bedrooms. As juvenile as this reference may sound, the symbolism behind it is something far advanced that the law enforcement profession has sadly let slip by, instead of taking advantage of mimicking the tactics for a beneficial impact. Suppose a politician was to claim an absolute or solidified position on a specific topic, even though they once swore allegiance to a complete contradiction. In that case, that same politician can state that they have changed perspectives due to some catalyst or revelation of new knowledge.

While the entire audience can be seen hiking up their pants because the bullshit is getting deep, the politician offers the salesman's smile, two thumbs up accompanied by a corny joke, and voila'; the past is the past, and let's move on.

I don't oppose Roman Catholicism, nor do I believe all politicians are insincere. By using these topics for illustration, I only wish to highlight my sense of twisted envy for them being able to survive in the face of what some would state to be inevitable extinction. Like law enforcement, both models should be held to a "higher standard"; however, upon the occurrence of a falter from that standard, they are commonly granted a "do-over". This trend is not attributed to their uncanny ability to offer sincerer or more heartfelt apologies than would be that of police officers. This trend is attributed to the fact that they have

mastered turning the page, whereas the police professionals read the same page, counteracting the fact that
history has indicated that this tactic does not work.
Instead of turning that symbolic page of an event, law
enforcement seems to consistently see the end result of
ripping the page from the book and begging the public to
slice us with it. Political patronization and organized religion are comprised of faith-based followers who will maintain their following by their trust in the applicable system.
That is the basic definition of faith, and society should
have faith in law enforcement, despite us having our transgressions as the comparisons chosen herein.

THE LESSON HERE:

Can't beat em, join em.

*Law enforcement could easily enjoy this same benefit, as most
everyday people are law-abiding and have a vested interest in
law and order. However, we've provided our reasons to the
masses why they should not grant us this benefit. The majority of
everyday people have faith in the same objectives and standards,
which are descriptive of the law enforcement profession. This
faith should not be exploited by law enforcement but instead
embraced so that the profession can be allowed to operate with
confidence.*

When a police officer goes from 'protector' to 'defec-
tor' – the national discourse is usually padded with expla-
nations, apologies, and other countermeasures. When

Officer Smith with the Wherever Sheriff's Office is caught falsifying arrest reports, officers far and wide are quick to explain, almost rationalizing the act – "well the judicial system is backward," "it's a clerical error," "that criminal deserved worse." I've been privy to several conversations within law enforcement networks, where this identical behavior, on the part of police antagonists, is looked upon with harsh criticism as the underlying event did not occur anywhere close to the proximity of the antagonists' fury. Officers can be heard relaying questions and statements representing this belief. Why are they protesting here? Why are they against us? In such a warped sense, police officers, especially leaders, emulate the behavior of those they criticize most. Law enforcement channels will openly admit the perplexed stare that occurs, from within the ranks, when murals of alleged victims of non-adjudicated excessive police force are constructed within their respective areas, as the brick buildings where the graffiti is now artistically placed are galaxies away from where the incident is said to have occurred.

The utterance of "What's that got to do with us here?" seems to be played on the "repeat" setting. While the point may resonate personally with you, I'd question why some officers feel the need to construct their own social media-style murals of beliefs and opinions on these same incidents, given the same distance of relation to them. For some leaders, the opportunity to present a slogan as an outward display of opposition to poor police behavior is irresistible, despite the lack of any parallel to that leader's organization or demographic—hypocrisy at its finest.

The severity of the consequence of this guilt complex

has been felt not just throughout law enforcement agencies but also on the psyche of officers and the familial and social dynamics outside of the profession. Two of the most notable effects have been the unfounded allegation that somehow silence automatically assigns complicity or denies altogether an officer's existence being an officer to all family and friends. As far as the first effect, it is not only understandable but also required of police leaders to provide a condemnation of one of their own when that one has violated the public's trust if they are to have any chance at preserving that same trust, which can take decades to establish initially.

My point is that we feed into ignorance when confronted with the fact that if we do not publicly speak out against the actions of an officer-involved in an isolated incident, lands away from home, that we are in some way in agreement with the actions involved and not offended by the violation itself. Instead, we should use the resolution strategies I relayed from my church experience, in that we need to trust the system, keep the faith, and not judge all for the actions of one. The second effect of denying the existence of the officer's profession can have severe effects on mental wellness. As a credit to the apologetic culture we've created, officers nationwide have often turned to hiding who they are and what they do out of fear of reprisal, retribution, and collateral outlandish behavior targeted toward their loved ones.

When this strategy almost became tolerable, officers were then faced with the next level of this dilemma. Now some family and friends chose to disassociate themselves due to the involvement with the profession of policing and their need to cut that tie. I know too many officers who have lost relationships because of the profession's negative connotations. In turn, this has caused their remaining relationships to all too often set boundaries of similar denials or "do not go there" in terms of casual conversation on ideologies.

The creation of the pre-game speeches has become prevalent now, in terms of officers receiving the lecture of "Do not talk about your job" before arriving at their intended destination for social gatherings. Beaten spirits cannot endure isolation, so the result is often adherence to these boundaries as a sole means of preservation of these relationships. For this situation, I only wish we could be treated as politicians, in that we can admit to having changing perspectives with what we know now, compared to what we only knew then, and then move on to the "next question" while holding two thumbs up and offering a contagious smile.

THE LESSON HERE:

Stop and pay the toll.

Always bear in mind the toll of the profession we CHOSE has on our loved ones. For every one incident they tell us, there are dozens more, in which they have been degraded, disrespected, or demoralized, simply by their close connection to us. It's not fair, and it will never be. For this reason, with all of your might, honor them for this. Love them, like they love you, and know that you do not bear the cross alone.

When the dark sides of society present themselves center-stage, leaders can bury their heads so far into the sand that they will finally reach water and drown themselves, or they can lead. As cliché as the term "lead" may sound, the spirit behind the action and the intended impact is paramount.

Leaders can shout from the rooftops of their respective departments, for all to hear, that society's failures are wrong, not try to create a route for appeasement, which only gifts their people with free targets on their backs. Leaders can show their people the self-sacrifice of being the outside cynic's target while not abdicating their duties and responsibilities by stating facts and the harsh reality of those facts. Simple facts could be easily provided that would, at the very least, provide vital information as to why officers did what they did or do what they do daily.

Providing these facts does not come with a stamped guarantee of a holiday greeting card from those who will continue to oppose; however, even without the formation of a friendship, we can at least plant the seeds for understanding. I routinely welcome opportunities to inform would-be complainants of police procedure and constitutional authorities afforded to law enforcement, to which I make sure to highlight the fact that they will probably not like what I'm about to tell them. By stating the obvious, which is read by their predisposition to oppose anything besides their own free will, they often acknowledge that they do not like it.

Still, they can agree that it is the law, policy, or procedure shown in this fashion. I've provided copies of constitutional laws. The most frequent of these informal debates would be attributed to officers' ability (at least in New Jersey) to have the drivers of vehicles, subjected to a lawful stop, exit the vehicle without any further justification or requirement. Between this and the verbiage about relative statutes of resisting arrest, most oppositionists cannot fathom this to be true without viewing it for themselves. Even then, on occasion, they will persist in debate, but I can least know that they were provided the unbiased, factual basis of my statements to them. I usually end the session because I did not compose the law but know how to follow it.

LESSON:

We agree to disagree.

Even if you bring a counterpart to an oak tree and explain that it is a tree, they may still argue and call it a large plant. If your goal is to get counterparts to nod in agreement, you often are not approaching the situation with realistic expectations. You can, however, shock the conscience and treat the counterpart to the information they usually are never given out of understandable frustration on the part of the police profession. Nothing fits the general public's viewing pleasure as much as when an officer professionally provides accurate information on the law, order, and procedure, to someone adamant on the countersubject. Treat these moments as teaching moments. Expecting agreement from the resident across from you is ideal yet not practical. They're emotionally charged and angry while you're professional and calm. Strive to meet them in the middle with facts, logic, and law.

Police leaders often miss, sometimes once-in-a-career opportunities, to shine when they are faced with extreme adversity. Simple facts can serve as a flotation device during these times by adhering to the basic principles that surround us and our profession. For instance, if officers are required to use a certain level of justifiable force to effectuate an arrest, it will probably not be visually appealing to civilians, nor was it ever intended to be.

The fact is we are equipped with various tools that would not be categorized as anything else than for which they are intended. I do not intend to spark the debate about what we need to be comparing to what we like to have in terms of equipment, but the mirage presented about this equipment only serves as a cancer to our cause. I was recently apprised of a department, which is now entertaining the notion of officers concealing their duty weapons from public view not to appear too overbearing.

This is precisely the notion of the cancel culture; we don't like guns, so cancel guns. We don't like cops, so cancel cops. This so desperately needs to be changed to avoid further calamity by continuing to travel down this slippery slope of never-ending false appeasement.

The ability to admit wrongdoing and exhibit genuine empathy is among the most noteworthy characteristics of an individual, not just officers. As in every profession, we have and will continue to have failures. Failures on behalf of personnel and failures resulting from logistics are a reality, as is the reality that the positives far outweigh these negatives.

The temptation to provide apologies or rationalizations for actions beyond any scope of our control needs to be curtailed, not avoided at all costs. I am not suggesting that forever mute our experience-based opinions. I am suggesting, however, that we not impulsively rush to advertise our stance on everything and everywhere at the expense of our personnel.

We've become prone to so readily offer apologies for certain aspects of our existence. Yet, we've neglected to provide that same genuine sentiment toward our fellow officers or, more deserving, our loved ones.

FINAL LESSON:

The sun will come out tomorrow.

We should never stop acknowledging our flaws, mistakes, errors, or omissions. However, as in so many other industries, we should also learn to turn the page while relying on the fact that our profession's core is dedicated to selfless service, preserving peace at the forefront of officers' minds. For every occurrence of a negative, there should be announcements of multiple occurrences of positives. If we focused similar amounts of our advertising energy on the positives, our plausible responsibility to apologize for our negatives would significantly minimize our profession's guilt complex. Transgressions provide opportunities for measurement of effectiveness, voids, and the potential to improve.

CHAPTER 5

Resiliency

The wholeness of the officer's soul who has just embarked on the career is something that should be considered as precious, for its sweet innocence has yet to be deteriorated by the public's abuse, the horrific sights, the adrenaline highs and lows, or the advent of administrative incompetence. One can certainly argue that the pureness of a soul becomes instant prey once exposed to the predatory world abound, no matter the path chosen. I've often admired a child's view of a dilemma and how they seem to have an uncanny ability to shrug that same dilemma off with ease.

As a more similar comparison equation to law enforcement, a societal consensus exists about how a soldier will undergo unavoidable transformations to serve the nation abroad. Law enforcement officers are "deployed" domestically for decades yet have not been afforded the adequate resources to counteract the soul transformation that accompanies these deployments. In the spirit of fairness, how can this soul evolution be consistently measured in a manner to earn the cooperation of the measured masses?

Unfortunately, online retailers have yet to market a viable instrument capable of measuring the amount of deterioration that actually occurs or how and when it will inevitably take its course. We have realized that, although we are "good" at many things, being more aware of the warning signs associated with "at-risk" officers was one thing definitely in need of vast improvement. Without further ado, we enter the new era of how to address this: The Resiliency Movement.

One loose definition of resilience is a capability to bounce back from a source of difficulty or internal challenge. Just as there are significant variations in policing tactics, so would be the case in how and what can affect individual officers. Science and experts will continue to invoke their hypotheses about how one officer, involved in several shootings, remains unscathed. At the same time, someone who may not have been chosen for a promotion can slip into the deepest of despair.

The connection of officers to that of their human core and vice versa is paramount to the study of this phenomenon. Although officers routinely experience situations, which would be considered extreme or perverted to the average viewer, those officers cannot shed the fact that underneath their uniforms remains all remnants of an average human being, with human emotions and human physiological reactions. Connecting and evaluating these "field emotions" to human origins, not an industry (law enforcement), would be the very first adjustment I'd

emphatically recommend as an adaptation to this movement. While this may sound basic, it is readily discarded in
practical application, but then simultaneously critiqued
when instances are propped to the public audience, often
distorted in terms of comprehensive angles, which suggest
an inhumane treatment on behalf of officers toward the
civilian(s) recipient.

I can easily recall the heartfelt moment, collectively
shared, at the memorial services for a local officer, who had
been fatally shot in the line of duty—callously murdered,
remorselessly shot in the face by a gun-wielding gang
member, in broad daylight. Despite having the pleasure of
meeting this fallen officer when he was only a cadet and a
few fond memories of those times, I could not shed the
images of his lifeless body from being his lasting image in
my brain. As tears ran down my cheek, a news reporter
near our formation asked me why this was such an "emotional event."

The reporter asked if I was having difficulty with
containing my composure or my ability to now "perform
the job." I am now thankful for some of the mistakes I've
made over the years, how I used to allow such an inquiry to
incite a sometimes inappropriate response. I immediately
identified the motivation behind the inquiry as an open
invitation to provide rationalization that we, the police,
have difficulty containing our emotions as if our hearts are
eradicated or suddenly placed into sleep mode when we
don our uniforms. I used to wonder why the public would
expect this of officers, but I've come to understand and
recognize precisely where they've acquired this belief.

A LESSON PRESENTS ITSELF:

Why in the world?

Our overall wellness exponentially improves when we make genuine attempts at understanding certain things that upset us. Understanding and agreement are very distinct and do not have to point toward submission automatically. Law enforcement officers have been assigned a sense of expected emotionless service, so we cannot act surprised or become insulted when outsiders expect the same. Yet again, this represents another missed opportunity to enjoy a benefit branded onto other industries. As physicians delivering terminal diagnoses are often gifted an allowance of understandable dull bedside manner or separation from the patient, we in law enforcement do not allow the same tolerance for our field personnel.

For any "resiliency" based initiative to be valid, it cannot be based upon a sense of acceptance by our own channels, for what I refer to as "selective resiliency." Officers cannot be expected to abide by a moral code or standard of conduct that allows the influence of emotion in one setting (notable sadness at the senseless killing of an officer), but yet be critical of that same officer who may express signs of similar emotional response to another setting (let's say the senseless killing of a child for instance).

Unfortunately, we've created an environment in which the first scenario brings with it a sense of solidarity and understanding. In contrast, the latter yields that officer to various oversight channels or concern for their fitness to perform in the field as questionable. They cannot shield their personal distraught in a particular setting, which would be a common reaction exhibited by most others.

One of the most prevalent talking points of current societal circles is that officers are relied upon as stewards of their communities while representing that respective community. We are expected to abide by a set of behavioral and social standards which comply with the "most people" model. As can be referenced in overly-relied upon psychological assessments, which administrators use as fail-safes, officers at various career stages have their personality profiles examined based upon how their thought processes align with "most people".

From prospective recruits to promotional candidates, law enforcement agencies have become reliant on the field of psychology to serve as our partnered fortune-tellers of future behavior predictions and patterns. Like a fresh trail of blood in the water is to a shark, so would be any indication of extremes (to the right or the left) of the centric response, for the assessing psychologist. If such an extreme is noted, the psychologist will then sound the relative administrative alarm.

THE LESSON HERE:

Don't press that button!

From this point is born the foundation of frustration in so-called officer resiliency; we should align with what "most people" think and feel because we, the police, are supposed to be "most people" ourselves. That is until we act like "most people," which is when the floodgates of criticism blast open. Many of the polarized issues between non-trusting communities and the law enforcement officers serving them could be overcome if a pact was established to allow for the "most people" standard to be applied to both sides equally. Most people in the community are good-natured, as are most of the officers serving them. And in the most simplistic view, what aggravates "most people" also aggravates the police, and what pleases "most people" also pleases the police.

Resiliency should not only be taken seriously but should be applied by officers at all levels, respective of their backgrounds. The forthcoming suggestion, tactic, or recommended procedural change may not be traditional, but this approach's impact cannot be denied in terms of potential.

Experts come in all shapes and sizes, with some being more camouflaged as department wallpaper than others. Lackluster outward appearance, void of neon signs flashing their celebratory accomplishments, will often cause this class of officers and their potential value to be discarded despite the significant impact they can offer. Perhaps their expertise is relevant to parenting, caring for an individual with a terminal illness, religion, community service initiatives, etc., yet none of it lands on primetime television. Shouldn't these "experts" be part of the larger equation?

Administrations never encounter a shortage of these "experts" when their officers are involved in a fatal shooting, for instance. Based upon their previous-similar experiences, these steadfast professionals stand at the ready, prepared to respond to a neighboring agency at a moment's notice of such an occurrence; they offer insight, empathy, shared sentiments, and a path forward. Not to negate the importance or commitment in which civilian mental-health professionals willingly offer, but when polled, officers will routinely prefer to confide in those who can personally attest to their strife as comrades within the badge-holding community. As this resolution strategy referenced has become the accepted and preferred approach to incidents such as an officer-involved-shooting, there is no plausible explanation as to why we do not use a similar approach to other events, which can threaten an officer's sense of resiliency, and occur at a much more staggering rate than that of the previously mentioned shootings.

While the adrenaline-charged pursuit of a high profile fleeing felon, which ends in an officer's heroic justified and necessary use of force, may be the preferred topic of conversation, these scenarios are far from ordinary than the daily experiences that degrade resiliency within our profession. Family discord, financial woes, the death of a loved one, or health complications highlight just a few; these issues are commonly shared amongst colleagues daily yet are rarely afforded their due attention. In this current era of advertised resiliency programs, most agencies who offer any assistance program to address some of these will routinely see officers participate only under the guise of being "voluntold," administrative obligation, or anonymity, which is based on fear of what's next to come. Simply stated, an officer has to be resilient to participate in the resiliency program itself.

To counteract this phenomenon, I recommend that we identify and duly recognize officers who have exhibited less glorified forms of resiliency, which display the proofs of recovery upon the grimaces of their faces while never being the recipient of a formal accolade at a banquet. No, these officers do not wear the colorful ribbons upon their chest to designate their specialty yet have physically walked the path of their expertise. Choosing an officer as a mentor, who has just recovered from a grim medical diagnosis, to counsel others experiencing similar circumstances would serve the resiliency deities far greater than that of a distant expert source, with whom no personal connection can be formed through a virtual meeting platform. The caveat to this approach is that our law enforcement leaders need their fingers to be on the pulse of their people and not on the keyboard of their computers.

THE LESSON HERE:

Choose a diamond in the rough.

Leaders need to know their people, not just to the extent that their people will tell them what's going on, but to the extent that they can readily notice a change BEFORE something terrible

*happens. The commitment to learning and being an empathetic
leader is key to one's ability to recognize silent calls for assistance.
If a leader fails at this, then it becomes incumbent on a buddy-
officer to do so. Yes, it is and should be the leader's responsibility,
but it cannot be neglected by peers simply because the leader chose
to ignore it. If that occurs, then we ALL fail. Experts are
amongst us in all facets of the profession and life as a whole.
They come in all shapes, sizes and from diverse backgrounds.
Our egos often act as blindfolds in our ability to recognize these
experts amongst us, as they may not be of a ranking status within
our agencies.*

We all maintain a cache of personal knowledge of other
officers' doings and happenings as if we are part of a secret
society, the keepers of sacred gossip and sexy dirt. Think of
the last conversation in which you found yourself speaking
or hearing about another officer's home life and details of
such, which you know all too well that you should not be
privy to. Like me and sadly but true, I'm sure you recalled a
relevant example with ease about your unappropriated
knowledge of a co-worker's intimate dealings. This is the
basis of my theory on how we can manage resiliency much
more effectively by jump-starting the personal knowledge
vehicle, which we already maintain stored in our garages,
and placing it in gear on the road to recovery for those who
so desperately need it. Right now, we know of someone
who needs some assistance, significant or insignificant,
perhaps even just a phone call. A profound caveat to this
theory is a mixture of personal-professional courage.

THE LESSON ON THIS COURAGE:

Courage is a blend of the finest virtues all in one setting.

Have the courage to share your trials and tribulations, no matter how you think they may make you appear. True courage is the act of sharing these with the hope that you can help someone else avoid the adversity you endured due to the mishap, no matter if a personal vulnerability or flaw is exposed. The most valiant knights, heroes to all, held the blemishes on their armor as signs of strength, not weakness. The value of sharing genuine flaws, pain, or fears with others cannot be overstated in terms of the growth and the confidence that is bestowed upon them. When someone has failed to achieve what they set out to do, they have still gained something. That something is experience. That experience, although often wished to be forgotten, if willingly shared, may be the single attribute or contributing factor to someone else's avoidance of a tragedy.

This sense of courage also needs to have humility and lack ego's influence on the part of the officer-counselor. For instance, when I was a Lieutenant, I noticed an officer had undergone a significant change in disposition and the manner of his social interactions. A once jovial and proactive officer had now become an introvert. In a casual, "Hey, is everything alright?" type of conversation, he confided in me that he became aware of his wife's infidelity and is now involved in the initial stages of what will undoubtedly be an ugly divorce.

While giving the best version of a "bro-hug" I could muster up, I knew and admitted that I was not the right person to offer the understanding he so desperately needed. Did I care? Did I feel terrible? Did I want to help? A heartfelt and genuine yes, to all of them, but was fully aware that despite the attempt I would offer, he would not get the most value from my input or tutelage, as I was happily married for years, of which he was also aware. So instead, I arranged an informal and well-deserved meal (at my expense, of course, as it was the least I could do) with the affected officer, a personal friend/officer, who had gone through a nearly identical set of circumstances, just two years prior, and myself.

There was a method to the madness of my meal date and selection of the guest officer, as he found a way to not only persevere but to thrive thereafter. Through some tears, inappropriate laughs (based on some ill humor only officers can seem to appreciate), bouts of anger, and the admission of the anxiety associated with uncertain futures, a moment of true resiliency was shared by the officer simply realizing he was not alone or the first ever to walk this path. Sometimes, the most basic comprehension of knowing you are not alone can serve to be the most effective antibiotic for the resiliency virus.

Did the divorce happen? Were scars left behind? Are there personal voids left unfilled? Yes, again, to all of them, but these gullies were now negotiated by adding a psychological bridge that was built to assist with navigating over and through all of these challenges as plausible detour routes. Through the shared experiences, a relative association of an empathetic approach by an ally, a unique strength was gained, not neglected. I am personally proud to say that this officer is not only doing quite well but has also been more than willing to pay it forward in terms of the next officer in line, who may need the same type of broad shoulder to lean upon. I am just as proud, not embarrassed, to genuinely admit that I was not the ideal person for the particular job of counselor in this specific wheelhouse.

While the rank I held and responsibilities related to it would suggest otherwise, I chose to rely on something far more critical; common sense and how I would want to be treated if I was the unfortunate one holding my temples. I knew for a certain fact what my feelings have been over the years when being confronted with fraudulent credibility by someone who swore they understood, despite that being an impossibility.

THE LESSON HERE:

The golden rule has not expired...

Learn to place your inner self in front of your position when people need their personal resiliency reinforced. Treat people how you would want to be treated. The most suited person to offer guidance has earned their qualifications forged in their own experiences and sacrifices, not because of their uniform's insignia. Just because you may be driving the truck doesn't mean it gives you the right to truck over people.

Like many other new age directives which have become supplanted by others, resiliency programs can unintentionally become a "check the box" routine. While I have yet to encounter someone who would argue against these programs' significance, the honest energy often put toward them is subject to prioritization of a laundry list of alternate requirements governed by higher authorities. I vividly recall a press conference where prominent law enforcement officials stood at a podium patch to patch and touted a newly revised resiliency program's strategic implementation. It covered a myriad of topics, all based upon officers' wellness and increased chances of successfully preserving that wellness.

While patiently and eagerly waiting, I failed to hear anything spoken of the bureaucratic delays of the "legal process" which would apply to all officers eligible for this same resiliency program. As a point of reference, it is not uncommon to have an officer involved in a fatal shooting sit idle for several months to years while the process evolves, even if the event was deemed justified by independent authorities and investigators. Idle time is the devil's playground while also seeming to be the antithesis of what the resiliency program would hope to achieve. This fact, being well known by the same leaders standing beside the podium, failed to be mentioned, recognized, and most importantly, highlighted as being a fatal flaw of this system. The realization needed to be presented that in this perspective, the treatment is worse than the diagnosis in terms of officer resiliency.

For resiliency as a general theory to be taken seriously,

as a resolution or mitigation strategy within our profession, the actual contributing threats to an officer's resilience must be honestly presented and confronted. The current approach focusing on external occurrences or influences has its merit. Still, without a candid analysis of how we, ourselves, deal with the various intricacies facing the involved officer, it will continue to be fractionally effective at best. Using the illustration above about the officer involved in a justified shooting who sits idle for an extended period, the accommodation of counseling, therapy, and peer support is fantastic.

Still, all offered support loses its intended impact as the avoidable delays in the forthcoming legal and administrative processes sink their teeth into the newly rebuilt resiliency within the affected officer provided by the program. The affected officer, who has been habitually taught to believe that the appropriateness of the actions taken in the field will dictate the relevant speed of reinstatement to full duty, has no other choice but to doubt the legitimacy of these industry-instructed beliefs when such a prolonged period awaiting final adjudication becomes a reality. Once again, we face the battle of the titans, advertised policy declarations versus the reality of the process.

Resiliency has to be a living part of our culture for it to have its intended influence on preserving our officers' wellness. A resiliency culture, governed by humane oversight, stands to benefit the officers' wellness and the communities they swore to serve as a positive collateral effect. Both the conservation and preservation of officers' wellness are paramount to the success of improved community relations and the longevity of the officers themselves to enjoy a healthy post-career.

Reverting to the "most people" standard, if we continue to treat our officers' resiliency by simply checking a box (therapy provided, now onto the next...), our officers will, in turn, have that same rigid approach to the community in that as long as they present a fraudulent expression of concern; Box checked. When that happens, they've checked that box of "show concern," too, and now they're onto the next call that just came across the dispatch screen.

In terms of believability on behalf of officers to trust in these programs, we are creatures of habit and prefer tangible proofs. The association of the participant officers suffering negative consequences of becoming branded with a stigma for such participation was not created in a fabled story. In addition to some unfathomable post-program punishments (mostly disguised as informal sanctions), some officers have been exposed to re-victimization due to administrative fear that inaction of noticeable consequence is somehow attributed to the complicity of the ill-advised behavior. Instead of proclaiming their support for an officer, some administrations sprint in the opposite direction to avoid being associated with an officer who had their resiliency diminished, regardless of reason.

I've had personal dialogues with officers who have returned to their departments from various bouts of resiliency. The common theme as a cause for their pre-return-to-duty anxiety is how peers will receive them. After identifying an officer in need of help and providing such help, the preparation to ensure an open and welcoming environment for that officer's return is just as significant. These components are the necessary ingredients to a system that fosters open and active participation by the stakeholder officers and decreases the trepidation that currently exists. With hopes that the affected officer is now welcomed back, we can never neglect the importance of the commitment to this newfound wellness in the form of consistent follow-up. I'm not suggesting a formal routine is the method of choice. Still, an impromptu personal check-up can leave an everlasting impression on an officer by having them see, in action, the genuine concern someone has for them.

FINAL LESSON:

Rocky says it best, "It's not how hard you hit. It's how hard you can get hit and keep getting up. That's how winning is done."

The symbolic imagery of a subject officer lying on a leather couch spilling secrets to someone playing on their cell phone, instead of actively listening, is what remains as the thought of what a resiliency program appears to be to some police officers. No matter how fancy and digitally enhanced the brochures may become, the fact remains that resiliency is something that starts within the connection we build with one another and our family networks. Together, with trust at the forefront, we can take proactive measures to expeditiously identify and treat "at-risk" officers who have been subjected to a variety of traumas. It doesn't have to take place at a corporate medical facility.

Sometimes, with the proper players in place, a candid talk, cry, shout, or laugh, can occur at the door to the locker room and have the same impact as several formal therapy sessions. Resiliency programs are not about what you do; it's about how you do it. Pairing our resources and collecting our efforts with the affected officers' families should serve as the foundation of any viable resiliency program.

CHAPTER 6

B.O.S.S. (Built on a Slide Show)

T here is no single element seated within the law enforcement arena, which can have as significant of an impact (either negative, positive, or hybrid) as that of a department's leadership component. A law enforcement agency's leadership can sway the tides of the morale and culture at the slightest turn of the dial. Due to the gravity of the position, the operational level employees tend to readily assign preferences as to who should and certainly who should not be in these coveted spots. Not even ten minutes of law enforcement experience would be required for an officer to have preferences as to what a desirable "cop" boss would resemble.

Those who choose the career path of policing enter the field equipped with certain expectations of what a boss should be. These expectations are born and progressively nurtured in an officer's "pre-badge wearing" stages. It is critically important to analyze their origin simply because upon that expectation meeting reality, this preconceived notion is vulnerable to emotionally charged responses. Whether pre-policing beliefs are based upon the indulgence of cop-themed television shows and star-studded movies, social media, and internet search algorithms, or the fact that we allege our profession to be "quasi-military," beliefs are created. These notions then become molded depictions of figures that one would either desire to work alongside or dread a coexistence just the same. Whether expectations are unintentionally set too high, or one subscribes to a system of letting things take their course, a slide-show series of images are created within the officer's mind of what that boss figure is, will be, should be, or shouldn't be.

From the moment an applicant walks through an agency's front doors, the initial impression left by those in leadership positions can be a permanent tattoo precisely crafted upon the moldable impression of that applicant, depending on the matrix involved.

Regardless of the formality of the systems in place, officers of ranking stature in an organization convey an influence by mere virtue of their designation, active or not as role models. Officer candidates and civilians alike (even when civilians seek to initiate a complaint of sorts as their sole purpose for a visit to the station) have a predetermined notion or imagery of what those in leadership should resemble, both in appearance and disposition.

———

THE LESSON ON PRECONCEIVED NOTIONS:

Don't be too fast to judge a book by its cover.

These prefabricated expectations of those in charge are not unique to just policing, as can be seen through this phenomenon's noticeable symmetry throughout society. When an individual is adamant in their demand to "see the manager" at a chain-style store, a subconscious shift in psyche occurs, which can either be satisfied upon the arrival of him/her or completely demolished. All too often, unsupported expectations can serve to our detriment instead of our advancement.

The demolition effect occurs on the last fraction of hope when the individual's pessimistic premonition is reinforced, and the arrival of that manager is accompanied by a symbolic fluorescent sign that shines overhead, "I have no clue how I was promoted." The best version of this example is the military metaphor of a "post turtle," a shared image of a turtle sitting atop a fence post. All who view it know what they see; they haven't the slightest idea of how it got there. Rest assured, we all know at least one. Upon interacting with a post turtle or unluckily falling under their supervision, an individual's esprit de corps can be depleted at the speed of light. As the disappointment is exhausted through an audible sigh from the nose and mouth, so is the confidence exhausted of the recipient of that experience in that particular brand of store or police department the inept manager represented.

Satisfaction, often accompanied by an essence of relief

and assurance, is best observed when the incorporation of
a managerial employee almost instantly calms the rough
seas. The ability to quash a heated situation and settle
disputes is a highly sought-after trait of a leader. This
steward of the department's reputation is the preferred
choice to ensure compliance at all levels while simultaneously safeguarding the cooperative commitment to
customer satisfaction.

From my research-based and inquisitive conversations
with officers of various levels of experience, despite some
drastic societal changes through the decades, these initial
interactions with leaders all seemed to have a commonality: confusion. By way of confusion, the majority of officers
I spoke with, to include myself, all related to a vivid recol-
lection of meeting a picturesque police leader. Depending
on the era, this surreal deity of the agency may have rocked
a high-tight flat top with an upper-body shaped in a "V,"
garnered with unquestioned loyal support from all who
came into contact and left most in admiration of even their
shadow. So as I or many others would walk away, after an
initial encounter, with a sense of awe, that sensation would
soon succumb to other emotions as now a care-bear figure,
wearing a uniform suffering from exceeding the maximum
P.S.I. of button pressure, enters the scene. The only way to
officially identify this person as a representative of supervisory rank is to carefully inspect the wrinkled and stained
uniform for any noticeable insignia to designate such rank,
as the observer officer's limbic system is overflowing with a
sense of denial otherwise. So as we sit in the infancy stage
of our career, we are already faced with a problem of
disproportionate leadership imagery. One figure whose

own breath even respects him by always yielding the right of way and the other who prefers to hug a bug rather than swat one away.

THE LESSON FROM THIS CONFUSION:

Women want him, men want to be him.

Try to govern your expectations so that they have room to be adjusted. Attempting to eliminate all preconceived notions is prone to fail as this tendency is innate to humans and outside influences. Allow the formation of your opinions of leaders from what you experience and not what others "claim" to have experienced by their recollections.

If agreeably so and stated with consistency on most officers' behalf, about the significance of effective leadership within law enforcement, how could such a vital part of our profession be in such a state of disorder? The simple and most direct answer I have provided when confronted with this question in the past has afforded me a myriad of reactions, stopping just short of a punch in the face (although it's been close a few times).

We, the police, are bad at this leadership "thing", specifically in the ability to measure one's ability to lead. While we are not alone, industry-wise, we have to come to terms with the issue at hand in that we have a systemic leadership deficiency. However, although we may admit we have a problem, we tend to accept the mediocrity approach being there's not much we can currently do about it due to our deviation from the private sector in terms of impulsive changeover. Although some extreme examples may exist (radical and disillusioned agendas of dissolving entire police agencies), it would be a safe assumption to generally state that we are gifted economy-sized containers of failure repellants by various legislative bodies for our respective departments. This repellant shields us from the specific disastrous outcomes we would undoubtedly come to expect if our agencies were replicated in the private sector in terms of accountability at the highest levels.

My claim of a systemic deficiency in law enforcement is based upon, at least, for the most part, effective performance standards seeming to automatically decrease as the rank designation increases. While such coveted archives as policy manuals or directives may list "duties and responsibilities" in such a fashion that one would think an officer of supervisory status is flooded with required proficiency standards, the all-too-often reality is that once this status is ordained upon an officer, one is immune from recall even if underperforming is noted by the masses, with one of the only exceptions to be by committing egregious violations. In the private industry, if a person of leadership is consistently flailing their arms with uncertainty and only submitting sub-par results, a significant change is not only expected but to most would be inevitable. No such egregious violation needs to occur further than that of inefficiency or failure to meet a standard. Am I suggesting that law enforcement leaders be swapped like one would underwear in the private sector? No, but I assign a level of value to hold those in leadership positions to a higher standard than expected of the operational level.

THE LESSON THIS COMPARISON TEACHES:

If you can't beat them, you don't have to join them.

Despite what system of beliefs others may subscribe to, always hold yourself to high standards, especially to higher standards than those you're blessed to lead. I've personally recommended that they routinely mimic and emulate those in positions above them (deserving of such emulation) while also safeguarding their work ethic to be that of a manual laborer. By combining a sense of strong and physical work ethic and natural leadership behavior, one can be successful within any given assignment or role.

The failure to adequately prepare personnel for a prospective promotion or assignment is unfortunately at the forefront of why our industry is lagging in leadership progression and modernization. Throughout the nation, I've expended hours of energy inquiring about how various law enforcement agencies prepare or train their prospective leaders before such assignments or promotions. I couldn't believe the abundance of situations in which provided little to no training.

It was assumed the candidate already possessed the necessary skill set, evidenced by successful completion of a remanufactured promotional process, which presents itself like a tired version of an old rerun of a corny sitcom. The most common response noted was related to the candidate being offered an introductory course to management, generally about a week in duration, encompassing the "basic tenets" of supervision as they are culturally recognized and accepted by our field counterparts. Our culture establishes this sense of security. If we understand these basic supervisory tenets (which primarily focus on managerial skills, not leadership skills), we are off to the administrative races. Nothing but continued success should be in our future.

The issue with this monolithic approach is that it covers extremes of discipline scenarios and old methodologies of performance management. It only touches upon the practical application of leadership theories. It fails to conduct an in-depth analysis of the most prevalent topics leaders will have to address if they intend to progress in innovative influence within the agency. The most prominent void in delivering this automated training style pertains to the noticeable absence of any "how to" in terms of the leader's unique opportunity to implement meaningful change and impact upon assuming the newfound role.

Our current leadership training models provide instruction, especially on the anomaly scenarios. Let's use an officer-involved shooting again as if the supervisor on the scene will be the sole representative to proffer guidance or direction. In most cases, these extreme scenarios serve as a calling card for all surrounding resources to respond. I do not intend to negate the importance of training a supervisor or ensuring the individual's ability to adequately appropriate tasks at a high-profile scene in a solo capacity. However, when such an unrealistic emphasis is stressed during such training with no mention of actual personnel management, we should not wonder why our personnel consistently feel mistreated when involved in these scenarios.

TRAINING LESSON HERE:

People are the most valuable asset.

I've always felt that the "book knowledge" should be learned by the prospective leader's investment and commitment. The practical knowledge of the human resources component of their newly found role should focus on the candidate's actual training. A leader should not be focused on the tasks, but instead on those they will depend on to complete those tasks.

This theory is evidenced by how frequently the phrase, "All you have to do is pass a written test," is used when officers are critical of someone they feel is representative of a poor leader. This realization has never been felt as it has been with the current polarized climate throughout the United States. Those in leadership positions, who may have been coined an expert in one area or another, have understandably found themselves perplexed about managing their personnel through such tumultuous times effectively.

Traditional methods used to address performance issues in the past have been met with sheer resistance, in the face of officers facing assassination attempts for merely sitting in a marked unit or the reality felt the threat of being criminally prosecuted despite following protocol and performing their duties within the color of the law.

Extraordinary times call for extraordinary measures, but if the training that precedes a promotion is simply ordinary, we are training to fail by failing to train from the start.

The complexity of blending the personal side to personnel management is one of the most challenging aspects when compiling a proficient list of candidates for supervisory positions. "Acting" roles serve as a practical and foreseeable approach for reality-based training while | offering glimpses of ability potential and afford a candidate invaluable experience when appropriately enacted. By properly, I mean that candidates should be vetted before the current leaders' announcement of any given procedure. There is no greater compliment than to be selected to lead a project or operation without soliciting such assignment but by being chosen based upon the merit exhibited before. This is one of the truest mechanisms used as a reward for performance compared to being rewarded simply for years of attendance.

In some cases, individuals change perspectives and, while certainly capable, may find that they genuinely did not find the opportunity to lead others to be suitable for them. This is one way to ensure that someone may be proficient, is not mistakenly promoted or placed into a position. This mistake is not noticeably felt by the agency, as the person is/was proficient, but is certainly felt by the person selected as the extrinsic rewards were not worth the intrinsic damage to their prior level of job satisfaction, as they are now in a position which is not for them.

THE LESSON HERE:

What the hell did I get myself into?

Be careful what you ask for because you might get it. Research every aspect of the position that you strive to obtain. The best research is practical application. Some supervisors are squeamish when it comes to sharing what they deem to be the intimacy of their positions. Still, by proactively involving yourself in a day of the life, you can at least set the stage for an educated decision regarding what you are getting yourself into.

The best indicator of how someone will blend personal to personnel is by viewing someone's background with an objective and fearless perspective. Being objective can be as simple as having an appreciation for life experiences that are foreign to what we've become accustomed. Being fearless is having the ability not to be threatened by someone whose background may exceed our own. The objectivity requirement can be achieved much easier than the fearless requirement, as we are creatures of habit. For instance, a military veteran who has traveled the world and interacted with dozens of cultures, with each imparting a different and mind-blowing perspective not realized before, may fall in a ranking placement to a bright-eyed college graduate who may be deemed more suitable for promotion as he/she checks all of the traditional boxes in terms of scoring potential.

The sight of all the boxes being checked is quite attractive to administrations. That visual appeal of box-checking can cause our infatuation-prone instincts to override our rational senses when choosing the top candidate. In another perspective, our civilian influences can also serve as a benefit in terms of projected or predicted success as a leader. Being a parent, a coach, a spouse, a volunteer, or a survivor of a personal tragedy can all be used to provide a better gauge of a candidate's potential than that of a written score. Until we, as a professional and collective effort, commit to adjusting the current channel of the known and turn the dial to the innovative channel, we will continue to experience these systemic deficiencies.

LESSON:

Leadership is a jigsaw puzzle.

Jump at the opportunity to follow the theory of "Walk a mile in my shoes." You can learn something from everyone you meet, no matter their place in an agency or society at that. The best leaders equip themselves with pieces of several peoples' experiences to use at their own expense when the need arises. So much more can be said of the person than can be said of the rank. Just because someone may not be at the pinnacle of the organization's hierarchy does not mean they cannot be at the peak of another entity outside law enforcement. Don't discount these people or the knowledge they can impart based upon false impressions misconceived and disproportionally assigned by you.

Bosses can be born from the most peculiar and unexpected situations, despite what the chapter's title suggests, in that we build what we expect a boss to be from a slide show of ingredients. "Real authority" is that of the genuine influence someone has over others and cannot be confused with "statutory authority" as in what the organization's policies dictate in terms of the authority assigned to a position's intended duties. Real authority is no better depicted than through the embodiment of the "indigenous leader". This indigenous leader is the one in the room who sets the tone for the agency.

Think of someone, who has no organizational authority by rank, assignment, or collar insignia, yet is informally recognized as the leader all the same. As informal as their official designation may be, this person has volumes of influence over those around them and often will be over-looked by administrators' lack of statutory authority instead of being fostered as an organizational ally. While all who know them feel it to be an organizational travesty that they are not in an official leadership role, in certain situations, the indigenous leader chose their path for their own reasons.

Nonetheless, their alliance with formal supervisors should be sought to foster an environment conducive to efficient operations while having morale at the forefront. In settings where all present can agree who the formal leader is, as their abundance of uniform brass can damage the cornea, all will offer the fraternal respect to the indigenous leader as they are recognized as the actual "boss", who all subconsciously follow in step.

Due to some of the systemic deficiencies mentioned herein, the indigenous leaders often find themselves at odds with formal management. These odds can be traced back to the fact that the formal leader is lacking in prac-tical knowledge compared to that of the indigenous leader, yet is afforded greater autonomy and desirable status bene-fits, which coincide with the formality of the position. Formal leaders need to realize that the indigenous leader represents a candid summary of what is occurring behind the scenes.

Their actions and disposition serve as a calling card that something may be lacking or, to the contrary, the agency is run as a utopia with morale at record levels. I've consistently said that if the indigenous leader brings some-thing to a supervisor's attention, which prods him/her to get up from the office chair, then it needs to be dealt with immediately. The indigenous leader can be the best confi-dential source to those in formal management positions.

THE LESSON HERE:

Calling all leaders!

Those in formal management positions should identify the indigenous leaders within your agency and bridge the gap to a cooperative partnership. If you find yourself somewhat of an indigenous leader, know your worth and carry yourself in a distinguished manner. Use your influence to positively impact the careers of those around you to invoke their focus on improvement for your agency, not as a sinister effort to thwart the agency's objectives.

Despite consistent remarks from officers in the field

and supervision theorists alike about the ideal leadership characteristics, we have still yet to embrace a strategic map to ensure that those most suitable for the positions are the same who are selected. I readily admit the legal boundaries and necessity for formal processes to exist, born from galleries of complaints, inequities, nepotism, political patronage, and fraudulent practices. The most apparent method to safeguard the integrity and foster an environment that requires those promoted to commit to a higher standard and continued progression would simply be to expose them to peer review. This suggestion is often met with reluctance and opposition when I add that by peer review, I intend that to mean that supervisors should be periodically evaluated by those they supervise.

The cancel culture would naturally offer a myriad of reasons why this would not be beneficial. However, there is no better tool to accurately gauge the effectiveness of a supervisor than that of the level of confidence they have instilled in those they lead daily.

This technique, when implemented properly, allows for a standard deviation, given the existence of the sour grapes and pucker lips, while providing a glimpse into the secret sentiment of the majority. It also serves as a preventative measure to those in supervisory positions from growing a false sense of a flattering reality regarding how the field officers perceive them as leaders.

While there are varying opinions, incorporating anonymity on behalf of the evaluator may reinforce confidence that honest responses can be provided without fear of consequence.

THE LAST BOSS LESSON:

A boss assigns tasks.

Contrary to what the peanut gallery would recommend, leading is everything but being a boss. When transformational behaviors are displayed consistently, the designation of "boss" is gifted upon an individual by those being led, instead of that individual forcing it onto those they are "assigned" to lead. We are in the business of people from all walks of life, who we encounter for all sorts of reasons, yet we tend to forget ourselves as people when we suit up for a shift as an officer. If we spent a fraction of the time we spend on overseeing officer/citizen contacts or matched the significant emphasis placed on how to treat the public and transferred that focus on how we should lead within our agencies, the results would be felt in all facets, with the outcome being a better level of service to those we serve in our communities.

CHAPTER 7
Thin Blue Line

The "blue line" icon has recruited symbiotic reactions from both sides of the philosophy for what has become a recent topic of energized debates and consistent controversy. The origin of this symbol dates back to the mid-1800s (with the color reference being red) when it represented a coalition of forces fighting against a concerted Russian opposition. In consideration of other historical associations, in the early 1900s, to both churches (thin white line) and even poetic lyrics, there is no distinct delineation of the formal patent or consensus of original meaning.

Research provides an informal agreement that suggests the first law enforcement references of the mantra being shared between then NYPD Commissioner Richard Enright (1922) and former LAPD Chief Bill Parker (1950's). These early references were based on an aligned metaphor that police represent the "line" between law and order and social-civil anarchy—that slim security device between the delineation of savagery and civility. As society's psychological and ideological shifts occurred, a relation to the terminology about a code of silence became prevalent and appears to date back to the 1970s-with the correlation yielding an implied understanding that officers would not report various forms of misconduct on behalf of a fellow officer, as a silent yet sacred oath.

The most notable conflict on the usage or belief in the meaning of this terminology is between the perception of civilians and the shared belief amongst law enforcement. Modern times indeed indicate that both sides remain steadfast in their belief, without much flexibility. We, in the field, can provide countless occurrences of officers reporting misconduct on behalf of other officers and being selflessly committed to the incredible task of safeguarding the public's trust. We, in the field, also take great pride in the fraternal solidarity that we assimilate to the profession, which can also be perceived by others as a commitment to protect each other, at all costs, despite public outcry for enhanced accountability.

In turn, this conflict fed the popularity appetite of the blue line phenomenon amongst law enforcement and its supporters, who choose to openly display large flags outside of their homes or highly visible decals on their vehicles. However, a boomerang effect, at the same time, has exacerbated those who feel it represents a negative connotation of officers bragging about minority oppression. As noted in Chapter 4, however, while this has unintentionally increased law enforcement support and various public displays, it has also simultaneously summoned the apology gods to find another means of infiltration into several administrations throughout the country.

Impulsive reactions to the loudest voices, especially in liberal regions, led to broad-based banning of the display of any form of the blue line by some leaders/jurisdictions, as the fear of association of the symbol to the basis of police vitriol was too much to bear. This knee-jerk resolution strategy exhibited did nothing but repeat many cardinal sins of the past; apologize without knowing what you're even apologizing for.

Instead of explaining what the symbol is intended to represent, we ostracize ourselves further by ripping it off our walls. Some are insulted to see it due to their interpretation. I am surprised that these same leaders did not ban uniforms and badges, as their public display clearly offended some. The ultimate irony, rarely if ever stated by leaders, would be the visible display of a blue line bumper sticker by a criminal offender to avoid scrutiny or interaction with an astute officer. I guess it's not that offensive in that regard (that's an argument for another day).

This chapter aims not to harp on the historical references, a contradiction of any one person's beliefs about the thin blue line, or to criticize the weak reaction by some leaders. The focus is meant to boldly provide some of the utter hypocrisy surrounding its common display compared to the reality of the application by our own members. For purposes of reflection, an average law enforcement officer's perspective of the thin blue line will be used by means of the thin blue line representing our profession and the pride that we share by being a part of it.

THE LESSON ON THE POWER OF TRUE MEANINGS:

Draw the line in the sand!

It is a symbol of a family that offers a sense of assurance, no matter where you may see its display in a geographical sense, to instantly recognize the familiarity to a brother/sister/supporter. The line that represents the commitment to lay down your life for your fellow officer, without fear or hesitation, while knowing they'd do the same for you or a familial association to same—nothing more, nothing less. Well, at least that is what we intend it to mean. While some have associated its meaning to that of the line between civility and anarchy, an oppressive air fills the room when this meaning enters the conversation.

The patron demon of hypocrisy within our profession thrives as it jumps from soul to soul, rarely exercised. I've preached that an officer's ability to achieve harmony with certain hypocrisies is critical to the best chances of not suffering from severe mental distress. From the fact that officers will often address and enforce violations for which they too commit, to the uncanny poise of dancing to the song titled, "Do as I say, not as I do." I view this hypocrisy in a unique way, which has stirred controversy when presented in public forums.

The fact an officer may conduct a traffic stop for a speeding violation, when prone to speeding, especially during off-hours, is in theory no different than the physician, who specializes in nutrition, lectures a patient on healthy eating habits, to only be caught in the act of devouring a fast-food burger. The hypocrisy of the job's duties with private practices is a fine line to be delicately balanced. The hypocritical officer allows a certain tolerance of expected hypocrisy, which does not impede on the oath of office.

The hypocrisy highlighted within this chapter pertains to the hypocrisy of culture compared to character. When the same officer, proudly sporting a blue line tee-shirt, is the same officer who damages a police vehicle, then tries to conceal their responsibility for that damage by offering the vehicle to another unsuspecting officer, to avoid consequence, they diminish the line. When the same officer, rocking a blue line sticker on their pickup, impulsively lashes out at a group of civilians and knowingly instigates negative interactions to incite public outrage, which now causes fellow officers to become targets of discipline, they diminish the line.

When the same officer flies a blue line flag at their home but is the same officer who deliberately violates the most sacred oath and commits a crime, causing utter disgrace for the agency, they, too, diminish the line. When the same officer, who tattoos a blue line on their bicep, is the same officer to engage in sexual relations with a fellow officer's spouse, again, they diminish the line.

I wish to emphasize that if we covet the survival of this symbol of our profession, we should also covet the foundation it represents. Suppose we are to identify with a code of ethics that codifies who we are and what we stand for. In that case, we must ensure that our behavior is in alignment with our professional obligations. One may ask what effect our behavior can have on our professional representations, but I'd offer a reread of the Jekyll Hyde chapter to sum that up. Simply stated, our behaviors are not isolated from public disclosure.

We, ourselves, have helped the symbolism of the thin blue line to be called into question, mostly in part, due to the behaviors we exude in our off-duty time. I know people who don't advocate for violent uprisings or unprovoked attacks on police yet certainly feel a severe level of hypocrisy concerning what we claim to identify within contrast with our actions. The "do as I say, not as I do" song and dance cannot be denied. I've only scratched the surface with a few of the behaviors which continue to diminish the line. I pose questions to officers throughout the country about their respective agencies' culture and camaraderie. Unfortunately, most identify with a selfish culture, compared to selfless, and relate more to no line than a thin line at all.

THE LESSON HERE:

"Great thoughts speak only to the thoughtful mind, but great actions speak to all mankind." - Theodore Roosevelt

No symbol or trademark trumps personal behavior and integrity. Don't feed the fuel for doubt. Don't just talk about the code of ethics; live the code of ethics. A symbol will only be an image of sorts and becomes meaningless if its purpose is not displayed consistently. In medieval times, many used a crest for the identification of a knight's following. The crest defined the bearer and was coveted for both its origin and the basis of belonging. The symbol of the thin blue line should represent those sworn to uphold it.

I recall attending a solemn service for a fallen officer with a contingency of officers from my department. The service for this fallen officer was to honor his life and heroism, to pay tribute to the officer, who engaged with domestic terrorists and was tragically slain. His actions and legacy were the catalysts for an overwhelming show of support by law enforcement officers from throughout the country to offer paralleled condolences. Despite the miserable weather of northern New Jersey on a December day, officers from several different backgrounds and wearing several different patches all shared a moment as if they were the same, from the same department and the same family. Like them, I stood beside the officers from my department and had an awakening.

I observed more thin blue line gadgetry and trinkets than I care to admit, while I, myself, wore a remembrance band around my shield, which had an embroidered blue line within it as well. Regardless of wearing one myself, I had this sensation I could not ignore, which overcame my emotions, in that something wasn't quite right; an epiphany of sorts. At that moment, I decided to treat the officers present, from my department to a gathering, a meal at the event's culmination. I knew that I needed an opportunity to share what I felt.

The service ended, and the collaborative departure from the city was highly compromised due to the outpouring of support personnel present. The city streets were mobbed with people and vehicles alike. I was so deeply impressed with that part of the day while simultaneously plaguing what I knew I had to do. As we entered and sat in a local eatery, I took the officers by surprise and confronted them, as I included myself, to convey the accusation of being nothing but frauds. I said we were the worst kind of frauds. I used personal examples of how we each had behaved on occasions to contradict what we just did utterly.

We just shared in a moment of solace, cried the same tears, felt the same pain, and all for the united cause; the thin blue line. We lost one of our own. We lost a brother. We stood shoulder to shoulder, embraced each other, and shared the sentiment of remorse, anger, frustration, and pride, all as a cocktail of emotions. It was tragically beautiful, the darkest brightness. It was the loudest silence. Yet, we all stood there as frauds. "Why do you say that?", one asked, to which I quickly replied, "if we could muster up such mountain-moving energy as an entire profession, such as what was just experienced, then why do we treat each other like parasites daily in times of normality?" I said when the procession has finished its drive through the streets, and the folded flag is gently handed off to the newfound widow, we head back home to reassume our position in the land of hate thy neighbor at a moment's notice for the most trivial of reasons.

I preached to the group that we should take this opportunity of indoctrinated beliefs and sentimental mood to impact our daily police lives and personal habits in a positive manner.

It's a beautiful aspect of our profession to know that if

a police officer was to fall victim to an assailant, they could rest assured their loved ones would be cared for to some extent or another. However, this should accompany another true aspect; a prerequisite to duck and dive out of the way of cynical shots being fired at "us," from "us," on the typical Tuesday at work with "us."

As a reactionary impulse, we've collectively gathered once again, in unity, to oppose the newly launched campaign against the mistreatment of officers and negative light cast onto our profession.

Still, I again challenge the police officer reading this book to change my mind about why we should expect better treatment from the outside when we treat each other poorly from the inside. When one wears a sign that says, "Kick me," one cannot be disgruntled about how many targeted kicks are felt upon the buttocks.

This model of indifference to humanity, of officer/officer interactions, has become commonplace amongst officers throughout the nation has to be confronted but must be acknowledged before any genuine or constructive reform.

THE LESSON HERE:

The first step is admitting you have a problem.

Acknowledgment is difficult, especially in an area such as this, but is vital to the efficacy of the wellness initiative. There is a significant difference between being a human being and that of being human. If treating each other, as officers, with basic

humanity, is difficult, you will undoubtedly have extreme
difficulty with the proper treatment of people in public or
private venues. There are various ways to evaluate the level of
humanity and camaraderie within an agency: Morale, level of
volunteering, reciprocity of sacrifice, good and welfare
initiatives, and the exchanging of common courtesies.

One of the most elementary tactics used to measure the workplace environment would be by the observation of personal greetings or lack thereof in terms of officer interactions. I've made it a point to routinely greet everyone from the custodian to the Chief of Police upon encountering them.

On occasion, I have chuckled in disbelief when greetings are offered. The offering itself makes the recipient so uncomfortable that one would assume you asked an intimate or embarrassing question.

I swear that some officers must have been raised by wolves given their disposition on how they react to a simple greeting or fail to offer even the slightest of the same if they are the first to come upon someone. Once again, we see the conflict with the meaning of the thin blue line when confronted with the fact of how much it could mean if we've made it a point to not even say hello to each other.

Beyond the lack of basic greetings, look no further than genuine congratulatory expressions when an officer is assigned to a specialty unit, promoted, or happily retires. On the personal affront, ponder the level of pleasure extended to a fellow officer when he/she goes on a vacation, buys an exquisite home, or purchases a sought-after luxury vehicle.

While I'm not a gambling man, I'd venture a safe bet that the consensus for the scenarios referenced herein would all have the common theme that we do not willingly extend a sense of genuine happiness when others are blessed in some regard. Blue line family? I say it's more like having the blues for our shortcomings or unrealized expectations, which were never reality-based from the beginning.

I've come to realize that not everyone is capable of overt displays of kindness or comfortable with social interactions. Some officers and people can simply interact with anyone without the slightest unsettling of appearance, while others have noticeable and uncontrollable anxiety.

Some officers choose a more private disposition and do not want others to know much of them outside of their title and uniform, which must also be respected. I routinely recommend that of "grocery line etiquette" at a minimum. While someone waits patiently to scan and pay for groceries, it is common for them to analyze the person in front or behind in line. Although eye-rolls may occur when someone chooses the express line while possessing enough food items for an NFL team, the ordinary interactions among consumers are short, kind, and basic. We are all capable.

———

THE LESSON HERE:

Practice makes perfect.

If we can practice common etiquette and personal decency in tranquil times, it will not be cumbersome to extend the proper care to others during times of tragedy. The foundation of good and welfare should be established well before it is ever desperately needed. In trying times or tragic scenarios, the relationships forged prior can be reinforced and strengthened by the shared reaction to achieving the common goal of overcoming adversity. Relationships based on genuine concern and kindness can serve as the ideal chicken soup for the soul when it is needed the most. Relationships should never be sacrificed for the acquirement of a tangible benefit. Relationships are the glue to a strong-willed organization.

Our profession and culture are unique in terms of how we act toward each other, compared to how we say we feel. In any multi-agency training initiative, cooperative investigation, or law enforcement ceremony, we send optical lasers of unspoken negativity at officers from other agencies as we examine our counterparts from head to toe, being critical of every inch. The hysterical part of this reality is while we do so, the subject of our appearance autopsy is doing the same to someone else! At any "community meet the police event," take note of how the officers flock together, as if some magnetic field binds them, even though they may not be "friends" and the fact that the entire purpose of their attendance is to interact with community members. There is a reason for these behaviors. It's what I consider to be that sibling love-hate relationship. We commonly will criticize and demean each other but will then staunchly oppose an outsider from doing the same while finding an awkward sense of safety and comfort when in each other's company.

I genuinely believe that the love and respect for each other are somewhere deep down, but we must allow it to surface if we ever want our thin blue line to truly represent "something." This "something" would be proudly professed and not subject to recall as we could unanimously state that it represents belonging to a family committed to the noble cause of selfless service. Military veterans, physicians, and even certain university alumni are allowed to visibly show their instinctual pride of belonging to their "something." I've never observed someone verbally castrated for wearing a "Proud to be a Teacher" shirt. We should be no different. We've allowed this negative facet and label to be applied to our profession. While we have not effectively controlled or extinguished the false narrative that has been assigned, we must also not be complicit with the false narrative by only strengthening its message by behaving poorly on the public stage.

THE LAST MESSAGE ON THE THIN BLUE LINE:

I am much more than a line.

Our profession means so much more than the symbol of a thin blue line. The traditions forged in the heroic actions taken by those before us and the prolific actions of those to come are what define us—the proud sense of belonging to something we recognize to be larger than ourselves. The symbol does not represent perfection, nor was it ever meant to be. The symbol does not represent an "us versus them." The symbol does not celebrate the areas where we readily admit we've failed and hurt some instead of helped. The symbol is meant to represent the pride of membership and support as we identify with being the sworn safeguards of the communities we call home. The weight is on our shoulders to display a true commitment to this message, which starts in our personal lives and translates into our everyday interactions with one another as officers. We can then establish the sturdy platform to intelligently defend the genuine meaning of the thin blue line we are so proud to continue to represent professionally.

CHAPTER 8
Green Grass

A dmittedly so, the words "if I only..." have been the preamble to many of my rants over the years. What I would eventually learn was that an internal concoction of self-pity and reluctance to embrace many of life's blessings bestowed upon me was acting as an anchor thwarting my smooth sailing to the seas of genuine happiness-that whole body sensation of serenity-energized felicity.

We've all related some time in our lives of vulnerability to the adage of "the grass is greener...," but I chose to truly analyze this phenomenon as I came to terms with the fact that I was plagued by depression, which was well within my ability to control. Control over the emotions, especially those that are reactionary, can be complicated to achieve, but mitigation strategies definitely within reach, which I failed to recognize were at my fingertips.

An admission that we have control over our reactions can be most frightful because, after all, by offering an admission, we also simulcast a sense of responsibility.

Anything short of controlling our reactions to the myriad of situational dramas we experience would be irresponsible. Hence, we fear admitting that we are in the driver's seat of how we react to situations.

We may not be able to predict or prescribe every situation we experience. Still, we can undoubtedly coordinate and govern our emotional reactions into a state of a consistent and rational response, therefore avoiding such negative consequences to our overall wellness. Such consequences ripen the vine to grow and nurture depressive seeds.

The "d" word has been the subject of many scientific, philosophical, intellectual, and therapy-centric conversations. Still, it has rarely been casually discussed in our profession, despite it being blatantly advertised on the faces of many officers in our direct company. I attribute the lack of attention on this to the fact that we reluctantly, if ever, admit that the typical meal break commiseration is flooded with indicators that some are suffering within some aspect of their daily lives.

Unlike the suffering that some officers and everyday people may have experienced, which culminated in dreadful or extreme outcomes, mine was more relatable to the consistent malaise and disgust in many daily occurrences where others would easily find some sense of pleasure.

Tangible proof of this allegation could easily be found in a group photo of some joyful memory, whereas I displayed a stoic reaction compared to the blatant glare of everyone else's pearly white smiles. No matter if stacks of these photos exist, we persist in the commonality that such behavior is normal or to be expected. This needs to be handled better.

We, as an industry, are more competent now in the relevance of ingenuity, formal education, and strategic leadership. Yet, the casual discussion of this fact is nonexistent, never mind actually addressing it. We habitually react to the worst-case scenarios instead of recognizing and handling the common scenario hiding in the wide-open view.

I can nearly offer a guarantee that if a random officer was asked about the last conversation they had with a colleague, the response would suggest it was not doused in joyful flavor, and wishful blessings being directly or indirectly tagged to each other. There would likely be no blissful thoughts of encouragement being shared on behalf of someone venturing out.

I genuinely don't have regrets in my life or career, but one thing has rung within the confines of my mind and repeatedly played like a broken record; I wish I knew then what I've come to know now and *did something about it*. The simple reason behind this proclamation is for the precious time I cannot retrieve in wasted energy and dismal moods towards my family and friends, who are the ones I love more than words can say.

THE FIRST LESSON PRESENTS ITSELF ABRUPTLY:

When there's less time ahead than what has been already spent...

Time is the most valuable thing on this planet. If something is plaguing you that is causing your time to be wasted on things that only add to your demise, eradicate its source. There is nothing more important than spending your time wisely. When you are in a constant state of depressive moods, you wish the time away, until one day you awake from the slumber of misery to wish it back so that you can have a do-over. Time is precious. Start treating it as such.

As I've mentioned previously, and the title of this book would suggest, the outcome of depressive behavioral expressions cannot and should not be a surprise, given the path this profession and its uninvited contributors have established for prospective members. Even when I was blessed to have been promoted for the first time, I inherited a salary increase that nearly doubled my income, yet the euphoric reaction fizzled in record time. Overnight, my financial position and status changed drastically, a change that if strangers were to be polled as to what they felt of such a financial windfall, would agree that it was "life-changing." Yet, for me, the truth is that nothing in terms of my overall mood changed.

I was right back to the cynical Tom and worldly victim, feeling society's ills only targeted me and my surroundings. To my family, to my social network, to anyone with even a shred of awareness, my grass was the fiercest green color in existence, but that meant nothing in terms of my persistent personal dismay, as the answer for me was to consistently seek greener grass. The slogan "woe is me" became not just a mantra but a matter of routine.

Enter the intense research phase of my life and career, where I decided to accept the divine obligation to figure things out. I recall the numerous self-talks of, "This can't be as good as I can feel. There's no way this is as good as it gets." I can state, with mixed emotions, that I had exerted so much of my energy toward positive change and enhancement opportunities for others that it served as an impediment to having an accurate grasp on my own universe. It was almost as if I was deliberately eschewing my opportunities to feel joy, in order to provide it to others. I became a martyr to the belief that doing good for others would also make me feel a sense of goodness, without the need for any concentration on my wellness.

I relate this behavior to investing in the stock market while paying exorbitant interest on revolving credit card balances. Transferring balances is a slick method to appeal to the visual senses when in actuality, you haven't improved your overall position by even a fraction. I soon came to realize that if I did not properly embrace my path of ingress through life's several doorways to happiness, that I could not wholeheartedly bring others along for the ride, for we couldn't all fit through these doors at once.

Brandishing my best version of a celebratory smile for someone while simultaneously having an internal fire fueled by the "must be nice" or "why not me" additives became commonplace. The other "d" word that tends to

work collaboratively with my type of depression, referenced herein, is that of "denial." The world, according to
Tom, was that Tom was jovial, the life of the party, the
loudest voice in the room, and the one to insert hope into
hopeless scenarios consistently. Utter denial and subterfuge
could be the only possible rationales for how the reality
was not being confronted. Those outward depictions were
falsely protecting the fragile shell within.

THE LESSON HERE:

Turn that frown upside down.

*The concealment of one's true feelings or the fact that there is an
internal conflict can be outright exhausting. Not even the most
physically fit individuals can endure a constant assignment to
fake mood exhibitions. While it is not yet openly accepted in
terms of admittance, this behavior is paralleled with living a lie.
It can rapidly deteriorate the spirit of any officer or person,
regardless of their profession. I firmly believe that this
exhaustion of the soul is the most significant threat to the wellbeing of police officers as a whole, as a trigger for the demons to
mount their attack while the soul is left defenseless.*

Not to disparage or degrade the significance of training
targeted at advancing the profession or increasing effi-
ciency in officer safety, awareness, and responsible driving
tactics, to name just a few. Still, most officers would
concede that the number of officers who have suffered or
are suffering from an internal plight related to unhappiness

significantly outweighs the number of officers who have been or will be involved in a deadly encounter. Am I opposed to ensuring that officers are highly proficient in tactical prowess? Absolutely not. My point is that far more officers recklessly place themselves into the risk gauntlet of daily policing because only a fragment of their whole being showed up attentive to their assignment, while the rest of their entirety is galaxies away, struggling with an issue foreign to their tour of duty. If you can relate to this state of mind, about the unrelated "work stuff" impacting your focus on your "work stuff," you know what I'm referring to as to when you physically may have been seated in a patrol car but mentally, you are eons away.

Facing the harsh reality that one more of "this" or one less of "that" will not proffer the key to paradise is often the most difficult challenge for someone plagued with this form of depression to overcome. All too often, sensational quotes or inspiring stories can serve as points of reference, but until the individual is touched by their revelation, no constructive change will occur. An awakening occurs when one realizes that their current situation is mainly based upon the daily decisions they make or have already made and that a clear path forward can be established once the intended destination is established. That is the key. The intended destination is a must to comprehend what fulfillment is meant to mean truly. Different people have different destinations.

A game-changing moment for me came when I had an accountant prepare a yearly tax return. This particular accountant only allowed me to even enter his otherwise celebrity-based firm as a friendly gesture due to common acquaintances in our personal lives. While he kept the confidentiality of his dealings sacred, I clearly remember asking him if his affluent clientele were happy, as I couldn't imagine any other possible predisposition for those with "no worries" as us self-proclaimed commoners of finances often referred to them. The accountant told me that, "...one would certainly think so, that is when you've earned eleven million dollars in a year, all should be fantastic", while he motioned about a previously addressed client. As he saw my reaction, a mixture of awe and obvious envy, he quickly added; what is not fantastic is when "you spend twelve million." He then related happiness to relativity and one's ability to comprehend their reality. He assured me that as he watched certain individuals' portfolios grow, so did their anxiety and inability ever to feel satisfied because, for most, they never had a destined goal in mind. There was never enough for some individuals because there was no cognizant awareness of whether "enough" existed.

I won't say I learned everything from that particular tax preparation (and for the record, I would still love to know the feeling of making eleven million dollars in a year). Still, it did ignite this sense of realization that happiness is undoubtedly relative to the individual. Society has helped the average police officer adopt a philosophy of the next "latest and greatest." We've become so vulnerable to fads and trends that we fail to recognize them as infatuations compared to necessities. This unflattering fact is the admission of a clear example of how society's tendencies have effectively infiltrated the norms of the law enforcement world all the same.

As I've stated earlier, the average police officer, like the civilian neighbor, wants to keep up with the proverbial Jones, as is the case in any typical neighborhood. It's just that our neighborhood is blended with the awesome responsibility of safeguarding the same Jones, who we've come to envy with unhealthy judgments. When this private world crashes into the professional one, the officer is left with the temptation to covet what they do not have and discard the blessings they do have right under their noses. What may appear as an expected outcome for every so-called reality-based, drama-drenched series on television, this unhealthy appetite can be severe in the realm of the police officer. The grass will be greener philosophy yields itself to the officer making irrational decisions for what they interpret as instant gratification at long-term preservation costs.

THE LESSON HERE:

Hope that two minutes was worth it.

If you piss in your pants, you only stay warm for so long. Constantly feeling that you are only one more whatever away from something will inevitably lead to impulsive behavior and knee-jerk decisions to fan a flame, not extinguish the blaze. At times like these, it is best to stop, detach, reevaluate the situation, and think of long-term implications for the immediate decisions you are about to make. There is no mystery why the phrase "cooler heads prevail" was coined.

Given my law enforcement career in the Northeast

(New Jersey), I was fortunate to work in a region that compensated its officers quite well, especially compared to the rest of the nation. I recall a time being amongst some officers, who worked over a thousand miles from me, and the conversation of applicable salary arose.

I felt immediately uncomfortable as I knew their salaries were not close compared to mine, yet the discomfort rapidly turned to a different emotion in that of shock. Despite what I would consider a meager salary, especially for the reverence I had for them, their incredible morale and admirable appreciation for their profession struck me.

Their commitment to the cause morphed what I had grown accustomed to in my home zone. For where they were from, pride meant more to them than the assurance of having the trendiest pair of shoes. As distinguished as I felt myself to be, I saw firsthand what knowing your destination meant when I was in their presence. By no means was knowing their destination meant to insinuate a demeaning personification of mediocrity or acceptance of substandard wages.

I'd personally put their skills and police savvy against the best. Knowing their destination was directly evidenced by their sense of unison with who they were and who they aspired to be as officers, which directly correlated to their characterization as people. They proudly wore the scars of mistakes, tattoos of tributes, and badges of their honor, in addition to the badges strapped to their belts. I purposely confronted them with what some "others" had as sought-after benefits to their departments, and regardless of the gravity of benefit, the consistent answer they would provide was that of "good for them", compared to what I always knew of, "it must be nice".

THE LESSON HERE:

Look at that. You can learn something new every day.

Some of the most valuable lessons are best learned completely unplanned, from unsuspecting persons, at unexpected encounters. Don't enter a situation with a preconceived exit strategy if an alternative perspective presents itself. You may, just maybe, find that you had it all wrong from the beginning. That's how you grow.

The ill-advised tendency to desire a greener grass in our industry can be studied with several examples of deplorable conduct, which all fall beneath the standard of expectation of sworn peace officers. From various forms of theft committed by those who covet more wealth to adultery for those who covet more sexual gratification, the voids of the individual are fed with these portions of poisons.

Often, the outward expressions of the coveted behavior (such as the theft or adultery referenced above) are disguises for the root cause plaguing the individual officer and causing the depressed state of emotions. Yet again, these unwanted actions and consequences could easily be avoided by knowing your intended destination.

THE FINAL LESSON ON GREEN GRASS RELATES TO DESTINATIONS:

Find your true north.

Know what you want and where you want to go. If you truly desire to own a private island accompanied by a personal jet, you cannot be disappointed when you learn that your officer salary alone will not afford you that. If you don't desire to be the atypical husband or wife and parent of the American-dreamed 2.4 children, then don't get married and pretend to live that life. If you intend to drive south, you don't enter the northbound lanes to see where it takes you, only to get frustrated later once you realize that you are moving in the wrong direction. Life does change, and I don't prescribe a course so rigid without straying from a lane. Life does not come with a set of blueprints or a set of directions for every obstacle. I do, however, prescribe a sense of internal peace with knowing yourself and where you truly see yourself in the future. This should be flexible. That needs to be a priority and individually taught to avoid the consistent coveting of superficial means to repeatedly add substance to a leaky core. The known outcome is never to be filled. Many have said that the true definition of happiness is feeling content with less, not always hoping for more.

CHAPTER 9

Reform or Refund

In the year 2020, we were misled to believe that the police reform movement is a new ideology or innovative. Despite fielding criticisms, accepting inputs from a plethora of non-police affiliates, being governed with directives, decrees, and legislative updates alike, some prominent police leaders will still marginalize our industry's significant reformations already undertaken before this climate. Ironically, unlike many other industries, common reformative measures for policing all too often are outsourced to non-law enforcement "partners" and then implemented without our stakeholders being offered a seat at the table. A table prepared for a meal is not equitably set if only one side has placemats prepped for the chef's delight with utensils.

As I will always be adamantly opposed to the overweighting of input from outside sources, I also scrutinize the assignment of the term "partner" to sources that appear to be everything but in tune with the spirit of our profession. Some may read the preceding statements as a declaration of stark opposition to civilian oversight committees and the like. I have no reluctance or resistance to readily accept civilian input the various aspects of policing; however, when individuals with no practical experience are afforded the responsibility of how a particular operation should perform or given autonomy for the crystallized formulation of a policy for us to follow, severe consequences and inefficiencies are soon realized. When I've been confronted with this million-dollar question about my position on civilian oversight, I often rely upon a metaphor that incorporates an organized sporting event, mobbed with fanfare. We've all seen or been within earshot of the reckless loudmouth at a heated game, who wears a billboard of poor physical health as their exterior shell, shouting at obnoxious decibel levels about what a player should or should not do. "Just score the damn ball!", "Backhand that grounder!", "Has anyone heard of defense?", to name a few. The hysterical sense of irony in such fanatic behavior is that the loudest voices would usually fail if they made a physical attempt at the specific action they so dominantly shout at the players. If the fans were to dictate the roles and calls for the players based upon their irrational emotions, how would that play out? I cannot help but have my mind magnetically drawn toward the notorious and predictable statements made whenever the police engage individuals with deadly force by gunfire. "Why didn't they just shoot him in the leg?" is a question I have personally overheard more times than I care to admit and, at times, uttered by otherwise formally educated persons. I, like other officers, must resist the urge to allow our frustrations at such ridiculous statements to guide our responses. Instead, we should be capable of having open discussions as to not only the reality, in terms of the near impossibility of such marksmanship, but to the fact that some prescribed notion of a predisposition of blood-thirsty officers just waiting to kill civilians has no basis whatsoever. Being prepared to use deadly force is part of the profession, not the preferred eager anticipation of those in the profession. As I've stated earlier, the officer's capability to have a rational conversation is vital to conveying the right message; however, so is the recipient of the discussion in terms of comprehension.

LESSON SIMPLY STATED:

Talk to the hand cause the ears ain't listening.

Talking at people and not with them is a moot point if the hope is to gain understanding. Antagonists, who only wish to instigate an argument or have their oppositionist message shouted, should not be catered to by the police industry's willingness to communicate. A true understanding of perspectives can only occur if a joint effort is brought forth by both sides, with neither being interested in an ulterior agenda.

Reforms should not be perceived as impending doom to the world we have come to know and have embraced. The strategy of protecting and serving the public should remain as the core, while the tactics should always be subject to review for adaptation when the need presents itself. Our tactics should require consistent review for relativity to the cause; otherwise, they run the risk of becoming antiquated and inefficient. Any viable industry should seek the constant pursuit of progression, having its vibe defined in terms of its culture and strategic focus. The issue at hand is when our specific industry is not afforded its due, concerning our endless commitment to improving. That is not my isolated opinion. That is an absolute fact in just one decade alone when considering how many progressive updates have been prescribed, implemented, and effectively incorporated by us.

Conduct your own self-analysis to recall even a few of the significant changes recently prescribed to our standard operating procedures. The profession of law enforcement has either remained in step or exceeded that of the other major industries (education, medical, and agriculture, to name only a few), yet routinely finds itself as the centerpiece of the debate table of society's so-called nobles as to being in severe need of the "next best" method. The failure to highlight and advertise this proud fact that we are committed to excellence has and will continue to expose our industry to cynical and ignorant assumptions that we are in some fashion neglecting to adapt to be effective.

THE LESSON:

Look at how far we've come.

Facilitating our own narrative and marketing how we remain dedicated to progression is our responsibility. Suppose we fail to do so or expect others to do so on our behalf. In that case, we will inherently be led to disappointment, inaccurate assumptions, and the implementation of inefficient mechanisms by outside sources. The simple lesson here is to control our destiny by defending our platform. There are no better-suited persons for this task than those who have the field knowledge, expertise, and the ability to deliver our message accurately. Champions of our field, who have been transformational in leading our reformations, need to sing their songs.

Change tends to be digested like the world's hottest pepper, no matter what the industry may be, and law enforcement is not unique in terms of our difficulty to swallow something new. However, what makes law enforcement unique regarding reaction to change in the environment is the significance of the changes experienced in our particular environment. Private industries may change their target audience or may revoke the promotion of a product that no longer suits their best interests. Change instituted, thumbs up, turn the page, and onto the next.

In the policing world, however, as the years have passed, we've been steadily force-fed changes that send shockwaves through our souls and can create severe ideological questions as to the legitimacy of what "used to be." While a slight shift in our uniforms or the graphics on our vehicles may be the topic of locker room banter, specific procedural changes, which policing has undergone, required drastic adaptation to how many of us have honorably performed our duties for the duration of our careers.

Suddenly what was illegal is now legal, don't penalize - legalize, what was taboo is now mainstream, and what was unimaginable is now a common occurrence. While heroic actions taken in the field are appropriately given their due and recognition, I've consistently said that our commitment to constant adaptation is what makes us exceptional and should be proudly proclaimed by our leadership ranks, civilian officials, and legislators alike.

Our assigned roles have expanded in a fashion that has outpaced our ability to adequately staff our ranks to perform the tasks now expected of us. The logistics now required can alone siphon a police budget, leaving little to no room whatsoever to cover the other vital expenses.

It is not a matter of if an officer "wants" to do the job, but more accurately, if an officer "can" do the job, given the myriad of duties and responsibilities of the current-day officer. I do not co-join the ability to perform the task at hand to knowledge capacity and relevant equipment. I do, however, argue the ability to do the job comprehensively when only being afforded the "Econo-package" of preparation and realistic equipment and time-allotment options available.

As I consistently use the private sector for comparison purposes, I choose landscapers as a model. If a landscaper was provided with only a pair of scissors and told to cut a lawn, it's not that it would be impossible, but obviously, he or she would be ill-equipped to do so effectively.

In turn, if the customer was then upset at the time the service took and the poor outcome, which both should be expected, the scissor-wielding landscaper would view the whiny customer as insane. The result of attempting a task completely ill-equipped should not be a surprise to those involved. This metaphor is no different from that of the current law enforcement dynamic. However, the outcome of disappointment that we cannot be the end-all and be-all still surprises some.

THE LESSON HERE IS TWO-FOLD:

What did you expect to happen?

Leaders, don't expect your people to dig a trench with a spoon for you, only for you to be frustrated at how long it took and how crummy the trench looks. Think about how much has been added to the day-day operations, compared to how much has been added to the capabilities of completing those tasks in terms of personnel, equipment, resources, and training. For officers in non-supervisory capacities, be very aware of burnout. The last few years have had an undeniable effect on officers' wellness. I will vehemently debate anyone who does not feel this directly correlates to the overabundance of newly added responsibilities without simultaneously making deposits into the wellness accounts. An officer's time and energy cannot just be expended and then replaced via a paycheck, infested with overtime. That style of nurturing is equivalent to that of a sugar rush, which may be tasty initially, but always burns out and leaves you feeling more depleted than you were, to begin with.

As part of the reform or refund debate, the commercialized slogan of "defund the police" has garnered international attention; even its own reference when spoken into our household electronic assistants speakers as easily as they can recall the current time and weather.

Sadly, instead of a prerecorded error message indicating translation and origin difficulty, definitions of this movement are now at our children's digital fingertips, or voice prompted requests.

There are many pillars of the defund movement. However, I'll highlight one major component for discussion. A foundational piece of this collective initiative is to divert budgetary funds previously appropriated for police use and reinvest those funds into various social-based programs, specifically those about mental health professionals and their frequency of use. The purported goal would be to deter police involvement with the mentally disturbed community due to the often distorted headlines of officers only resolving these scenarios by the sole means of using physical/mechanical/deadly force. In this utopian ideal, these mental health advocates would, in turn, be dispatched to address the increasingly encountered population of emotionally and mentally disturbed persons who are suffering from a laundry list of disabilities and experiencing various altered mental states. I find this theoretical basis of this approach appealing, but the reality of its application is amazingly ironic.

I have law enforcement acquaintances throughout the world. I have yet to hear a single one of these fine men and women offer me any resistance when I've questioned them in terms of their desire to continue dealing with emotionally disturbed persons. Is this because I and we are heartless scavengers only capable of seeing the right and wrong sides of the law? Of course not. Is this because I and we are incapable of de-escalation and only capable of exerting some force mechanism onto others for our viewing pleasure? Absolutely not. I can proudly state that I have helped leagues of individuals who have been or should have been classified on some range of the recognized spectrum of being mentally unfit, with calmness, compassion, and peaceful resolution void of any physical contact whatsoever.

The simple cause for the lack of desire to continue our expected roles of a social worker in disguise is the agreed-upon sentiment of these types of scenarios, amongst police officers being of a "no-win." Those of us in the profession know all too well that these subjects are often violent, reckless, and without fear of consequence or even capable of comprehending consequence. Whether they intend to be antagonistic or not is irrelevant when you are the one summoned to the scene by others (often familial connection), who are frightened beyond belief due to the unpredictable behavior being shown. Does the fear of the family members calling the police to the scene serve as an open invite for police-initiated violence onto their loved one? Emphatically no, however, the callers have somehow concluded their loved one is exhibiting behavior harmful to themselves or others, to the extent that they can no longer control. The expectation that the disturbed person will instantaneously be tranquil upon the visual observation of police arrival and nothing further is not only unrealistic but irresponsible to even suggest. This unfortunate reality only leads to a scenario where the police are summoned to a scene, not proactively seeking to find a reason to use force. In contrast, and on occasion, some level of force is necessary to resolve the situation, preventing further harm of many sorts. Hence, a no-win situation.

Those of us in the profession also know that if mental health professionals are available for dispatch to these scenes, they are an adjunct to the police, not by our choice. I, like many officers, have been requested to be first in line to these types of scenarios, by the mental professionals themselves (who volunteer to wait around the "block"), due to the volatility they fear may be encountered. This proclamation is by no means meant to insult mental health professionals but to call reality to this bumper-sticker movement, which has gained unsubstantiated momentum. Suppose the non-police reader candidly feels that the policing profession would rather be steadfast in their need to be primary responders for interactions such as these, despite having counselors willing to handle them in their entirety. In that case, I'd implore you to reread the passage. No measurable amount of ego, machismo, or ignorance replaces the tangible proof that the policing profession was delegated these responsibilities out of inherent need, not as part of a self-request. Without the delegation to deal with this segment of society and without being accompanied by adequate equipment, training, and resources, this was an inevitable failure. No police officer I have met to date would dare offer even a suggestion that we should stand in for licensed behavioral therapists.

An undeniable truth to this dichotomy is that we are a societal necessity, no matter who may or may not want to admit it. I'd love to experiment with deploying therapeutic unicorns, whisking magic potions, or casting laser beams that use gravitational pull to remove deadly weapons from emotionally disturbed persons' hands, all as viable options to avoid forceful encounters. For those that may patent such a product, remember me! With sincerity, I believe that law enforcement cannot discard the importance and potential effectiveness of combining mental health professionals with the efforts of police officers.

Until recently, law enforcement agencies were almost entirely depended upon to deal with these subjects, especially the homeless, despondent, and disturbed.

LESSON:

If you see something, say something.

Here is yet another example of how we've helped set the table for our own last supper. Over the years, we failed to highlight the overwhelming number of positive interactions, attempted suicidal saves, and successful interventions we have and continue to conduct daily, where people's lives were saved. In many of these scenarios, various mechanisms of police force could have been justifiably deployed, yet they weren't. However, those stats go unreported. It is only a requirement, subject to intense review and criticism when the police DO use force. For the non-police reader, I am sure the last sentence ignites the question of, "Then why can't all of these scenarios be handled without force?" The direct answer is human behavior, the behavior of both the officer and of the disturbed person. No two situations or scenarios or human beings will be identical in all perspectives and perceptions of danger/threats thereof, no matter how hard we try to claim it. To include; while some officers are only equipped with perhaps a high school education and can find themselves, fresh from the academy, dealing with a disturbed

*person, compared to years of college, internships, residency
assignment, and formal training, which is common for most
therapists.*

When debating the fiercest supporters of the defund
movement, we often fail to present the harsh reality of the
sadistic forms of violence often associated with these
scenarios. Using the slogan "crisis call" or "mental health"
can be overused and exhausting while creating a false
perception that a person suffering from a fever is dealt
with by the police dumping an ice-cold bucket of water
over their heads.

Instead, how about a scenario with which I am
personally familiar. After a verbal dispute within a shared
residence, a documented emotionally disturbed man
fatally assaulted his brother's girlfriend by nearly decapi-
tating her with a large knife and then tried to kill his
brother in the same brutal fashion. Upon police arrival,
after concurrent 9-1-1 calls (which is often the case in that
the police are summoned to the scene, not just out
searching for their next so-called victim), the assailant
then exits the home, still armed with the same knife he
had just used on his household members, and attempts to
rush the officer. The officer, now backed into a wall of
parked vehicles with no alternatives, uses justifiable
deadly force, shoots the subject, and immediately renders
medical aid upon him, despite being unsuccessful at the
life-saving attempt. Is it the officer who needs further
training, reform, or deduction in viable resources? Is it
the officer's department that should be defunded to
provide funds to non-police personnel to deploy the

unicorns mentioned above or show up with the laser beams?

I often agree with reforms of various typologies if they include a comprehensive bird's eye view of the subject matter of the reform. For this particular topic, perhaps a complete overhaul of our crisis centers that are either bursting at the seams or abundantly negligent as they release these same subjects hours after their initial placement should be included in the reform initiative. The male assailant, in this scenario, was a patient of various treatment centers. Are we to irrationally blame these treatment centers as well and cast our unyielding blame for this unfortunate death onto his providers? The "what if" and "who should have" series of questions and arguments can infinitely continue. This disturbed man "broke" that night. Why did he? Why does anyone?

Theorists, physicians of all sorts, and others to include police officers, can surmise this and allege all they want until the "broken" day or night comes. I realize that is not a fancy outfit to wear to the debate stage, or a headline-worthy statement, or something the media would lick their lips over, but as you know it, this is the harsh truth of the situation, widely known, yet rarely presented.

In hopes of a constructive resolution to this dilemma, we must ask how these persons could have also been dealt with by the appropriate facilities before a systematic discharge. I also ask how often facilities or practices charged with the responsibility of after-care programs fail to institute any organized oversight of their patients, ensure compliance with program structure, proper allocation/consumption of prescribed medications, and disseminate useful information. And no, this is not the atypical blame shift often attributed to someone or something's inability to acknowledge their shortcomings. A monocle view of this situation or one telephone on mute for a dual phone conversation won't serve to assist the change we all desire.

Refunding what and how we do our jobs cannot be understated. By only ever adding more to our plates in terms of duties, responsibilities, and expectations, we set the stage for that plate to bend, then ultimately shatter. Any efficient industry in the private sector knows full well that you cannot simply add another step in the assembly line and expect the same result in terms of production without tending to the other effects caused by the supplemental additives. I am certainly not opposed to officers receiving training on dealing with the emotionally disturbed.

However, I am in stark opposition to broad acceptance by our profession's leadership that upon proof of a receipt of attendance at some basic training method, we are comprehensively prepared with nothing further. It instead serves as a false security blanket. Suddenly, officers are now fully capable of redirecting a disturbed person from committing the act they were intended to carry out as if the officers have now incredibly become fluent in the dialect of the deranged. Refund our ability to complete the tasks at hand with poise, professionalism, and excellence so that we, as an industry, exceed the standard, not barely meet the standard.

As I've stated earlier, I do not expect non-police stake-holders to correct their claims that we are not a necessity in terms of scenarios with emotionally disturbed persons. However, I wish that our police leaders would paint the most vivid pictures (with a movie-like viewer discretion notice) as to what our officers routinely deal with in this arena. I wish that our police leaders remind folks that the prescription pill epidemic has only helped foster future mania syndromes for far too many. Now that the manufacturers are beyond wealthy, we have been dealt the fallout and consequences.

I wish police leaders would ask their audiences if they've ever tried to save someone who doesn't want to be saved, who completely disregards the value of human life because they are incapable of comprehending the value of their own life. I do wish police leaders would share the fact that we are not equipped with some magical remedies capable of imparting fairytale endings and that non-lethal force is a viable option but cannot ever be considered a guarantee of unchallenged success, as has been evidenced so many times in the past.

My wishes may either sound familiar to you or may seem as if I am delirious.

MY WISHES ARE BASED UPON THIS FINAL LESSON:

"Progress is more important than perfection." - Simon Sinek

We reform how and what we do all the time consistently. We don't stagnate. We do stifle our innovation at times. The ability to conform to the needs of our constituents is something

politicians say they do; however, it is what actually we do. The pace at which we reform is so constant and rapid that we fail even to recognize the awesomeness of it ourselves, making it the inevitable outcome of our critics as well, in that they too fail to recognize it. If we are to advance past this flawed narrative, we must start to share and publicly announce just how many reforms we've undergone thus far and continue to entertain. Are we finished because we've reached perfection? Hell no. But just like any construction project, political promise, or cancer-curing device, it takes time married with persistence and expected trial and error. Reform methods you find may have worked or may have failed. Reforms cannot be implemented at the expense of adding more to your gut, which then further removes another piece from your being. Refund the voids left in our industry, but more importantly, within yourself.

CHAPTER 10

Choose a Car

The trajectory of an officer's career can consist of many turns, peaks, valleys, and last but not least, the "never" scenarios. I don't believe in operating in extremes, either personally or professionally, as extremes tend to get exhausted and inevitably break under the proper amount of tension. I developed this book with a two-fold purpose; to offer a candid glimpse to the outsiders into some of the secret halls of the police officer mindset. More importantly, however, it was meant to provide a guided path to those within the profession. An approach derived and constructed with enhancements, not detriments, with experience gained not knowledge forsaken, with common sense, not ignorance, and a means to build wholeness, not multiply voids.

I often challenge officers to a philosophical challenge in which they "choose a car" in terms of their career initiatives and the methodology in which they intend to commit their efforts toward achieving what they aspired to be, both in the profession and as a person. I use a modality of personal preference that can be paralleled to a vehicle categorization. As some prefer certain makes for their style and performance, others may choose those known for durability.

One can purchase an everyday-driver style of vehicle today, which is manufactured to extend warranties and longevity at the forefront. This type of vehicle, if cared for properly and driven at its recommended 55 m.p.h. suggested speed on evenly paved roadways, without obstruction by daily traffic, can be kept for the many years to come. This type of vehicle can be the type to transcend decades of use with dependable turn-key operability.

In contrast, one can purchase an exotic, lean, mean, driving-machine style vehicle today, which is manufactured for the sole purpose of an exhilarating experience for those who dare to drive it. This type of vehicle manages to surprise the driver with each ride, given its capabilities in the manner in which it grabs the roadway, snaps the body against the seat upon acceleration and turns heads as it passes through intersections. This type of vehicle can only be driven in two ways: hard and fast. A vehicle like this cannot be expected to last very long as the brakes soon start to squeal, the fiberglass near the tires begins to melt from burnouts, and the rear end sounds off with whining from being overexerted by the smokey, awe-inspiring burnouts.

How does the use of these vehicles end? Well, the first grocery-getter never seems to have its final chapter or the "right time" to come to its final rest, as it can continue to stand the test of time. This is because it remained true to its genre, lived up to its mediocre expectation, and was never tested or even teased at the thought.

While having a bittersweet end as it wasn't driven too long, the latter choice can be given its last hood kiss by the driver with a serene feeling of the heart-pounding memories it leaves behind. The sense of assurance that the driver drove that vehicle as if it was stolen, pushed it to its maximum capability, and stretched roadways to their limits, offers the owner a sense of ease knowing that there's nothing left to prove as the keys are tossed to the next drooling driver waiting for the chance to sit in the driver's seat.

By no means do I suggest that reckless behavior leads to redemption or that "Papa was a rolling stone" should be the theme song for the ideal career. Yes, the easiest way to complete year after year in furthering seniority is to color within the lines and symbolically drive that safe sedan. The main issue I have personally witnessed with this chosen means of travel is the inability to reach the intended destination. The gut has never been filled to satisfaction, the gas pedal never nailed to the floor, and the blind adventure continues. It reminds me of the hamster perfectly content with spinning the wheel, despite making no progress. Put the name to the face. These officers aren't "bad people," but they have not yet hung it up, passed the torch, and at the same time cannot offer a sound reason as to why.

In some cases, they'll provide a financial rationale (divorce decree, alimony, kids still in school, etc.) to why they can't leave the field. In other cases, they'll claim to still "love the job," yet every officer they work with will adamantly deny that to be accurate, as evidenced by the actions taken over the words offered.

THE VALUABLE LESSON TO THIS OFFICER:

Just one more round.

Don't be the boxer that still believes they have one last fight still in them. Be the one who can leave the ring with nothing left to prove, at the top of their game, without allowing the fear of the next chapter to prevent the best reading of the current chapter. Passing the torch does not mean it has to be blanketed or extinguished. The torch will continue to burn eternally, I promise.

My criticisms of these types of officers, who continue to predictably place themselves onto the following year's roster, despite their expiration date passing in terms of engagement to the job, have adjusted to fall into alignment with my emotional intelligence.

I now appreciate that every person has different circumstances that govern why they do what they do and why they think what they think. However, as an industry, we do ourselves a severe disservice when we do not foster any normality in defining "completed careers."

Once again, we can look to our military connections for relevance, further than equipment, but to provide for a bountiful source of advice. There is no mystery behind the ideology of enlistment terms. No branch of military service offers an option or term of forty (40) consecutive years.

Have you ever wondered why enlistments are provided in bursts of segmented terms?

Shortly after the triumphant victory of the coalition forces in Operation Desert Storm, General Norman Schwarzkopf provided a rousing speech to a group of West Point cadets to illustrate this exact point perfectly.

Having gained international notoriety, the reverence of a combat titan, and the genuine adoration of those he led, Gen. Schwarzkopf keenly stated that he was in the "twilight of a mediocre career" and that his sun would soon set, yet arise again for the next in line.

He attributed this systematic leadership chronology to that of the "Army way," based on the belief that completeness and changeover were the keys to fulfillment and progress.

THE LESSON FROM THE GREAT GENERAL:

Is it my turn yet?

While many, if not all, would agree that he was atop the leadership summit as the pinnacle of the term, Gen. Schwarzkopf himself displayed a cool sense of ease, knowing that the next in line would never have the chance to realize his/her potential if never given the opportunity. In an ironic sense, this helped to complete his potential. Rivers never stand still, yet their moving current serves as the source of life for all terrains they encounter.

The human spirit or anatomy was never meant to

conduct monotonous tasks for extended periods or be exposed to prolonged extremes. I've often said that we should emphasize the importance of life planning far beyond the typical training settings that we have grown accustomed to, wherein we learn about a new policy or directive. As an industry, we have all of the opportunities at our fingertips to enhance life planning for officers, yet we act as if the clock of father time does not exist, or worse yet, can be paused, reversed, or advanced. What benefit does a retirement seminar serve, to those who are eligible, if there was no education offered years in advance to accommodate a smooth transition upon leaving the field? I'm an advocate for life training to deal with relationship marks (marriage, cohabitation), home purchasing, parenting, long-term care, and many of the other markers on life's natural timeline. I find the ultimate irony in speaking with officers, who claim to covet their pensions as the golden ticket to the enjoyment of the rest of their lives, yet don't take any progressive measures to ensure the enjoyment of redeeming that ticket. So what is the expected result? Keep driving that sedan in circles.

The officer, who abides by the career trajectory of the sports car, will undoubtedly experience highs, lows, and in-betweens. However, this officer's lack of fear of failure, willingness to explore new avenues, and testing of maximum capabilities affords them a gauge of the amount of fulfilled potential. It is not that this officer will never experience a sense of the haves, have nots, or could haves. Indeed, some of these officers know in their hearts that they may have been capable of more, may have been suited for rank, or may have been the one worthy of recognition, but were never in the right place, right time, or in the right circle of bobble-heads to the bosses. Despite that, they know the feeling of extraordinary because they shrug off the ordinary. They know the feeling of breaking a record because they reached for that record. They know the feeling of defeat only because they dared to enter the match, while others remained as spectators. Their memory books and tribute journals are filled with more of a semblance of a storied career than that of the quadruple decade career, simply by how they worked, not just how long they worked.

THE LESSON HERE:

Everyone dies. That's a guarantee. But, not everyone lives.

All officers will have their careers come to an end, but not all officers will have truly had a career to end. Having the memories of experiences you made, compared to telling the stories of others' experiences, makes all the difference in the levels of personal fulfillment. Make your memories.

Variety and the open-air market for variety in our careers are in dire need of repair if we are ever to rectify the diagnosis of N.E.O.S.; never-ending officer syndrome. As mentioned earlier, the plague of insecurities and fear of replacement within our agencies presents itself as a pristine roadblock for variety. I subscribe to a system of seeking out constant variation for the officers I work with, despite whether or not I ever had the personal ability to experience the same opportunity for myself. Having the self-awareness to realize your influence in seeing someone else advance or succeed in a new venture can be even more satisfying than experiencing the situation or setting out on the venture yourself. In a warped sense, this is work-related parenting, where you enjoy a constructive possession of their success vicariously through their experience because you nurtured it. This is yet another way to drive that sports car compared to keeping things status quo and not helping others to break the glass ceiling simply because it hovered over your head for your career. Yes, that next generation, comprised of those you lovingly supported, now get to that coveted penthouse floor, but you enjoy the invite to come along. Rigid adherence to what we know and what is familiar to us can often be the contributing factor to the lack of variety, not only in our professional roles but in our personal lives as well. This failure of confidence to taste new things ourselves can easily become what we brand onto others, instead of explaining to the next in line to go out and get the things we wished we had reached for ourselves. At the very least, if you don't have the gall to drive that sports car, hop in the passenger seat and strap in as a support guide for someone else's drive.

The most interesting and intriguing people I've ever met all seemed to have the common trait of ingenuity at their core. They always seemed to find a way to make the boring exciting and add vibrancy to any room they entered. The fact that they were not part of the law enforcement community exposed them to some of my first impression cynicism and typical misguided judgment regarding how their tendencies cannot possibly be applied to me. The preconceived notion that no one type besides one type (law enforcement) can impact our field is that tunneled vision that stumps our growth potential daily. What floored me was these private-industry pioneers would consistently tell me how interesting my job was, that no two days could ever be the same with the roller coaster ride of experiences, and how they couldn't fathom what we (police) go through. I recall being so perplexed at the fact that someone who literally travels the world abroad could think my job is interesting. This was just another slap in the face for me, as a calling card invite for me to jump in that sports car.

THESE PEOPLE TAUGHT ME SUCH A VALUABLE LESSON:

Let's spice things up.

Anything interesting, by nature, can be made to be boring and routine. The consultant who travels the world would experience no variety if he only stayed in his hotel room outside of the mandated scheduled meetings. If you decide to live in a box, don't be surprised only to see its four sides. Sometimes the most unexpected or unplanned events offer the most in terms of unintended outcomes and rewards. While much of what we as police officers do daily is scripted due to the nature of reactionary calls for service, there are abundant opportunities to create, innovate, and investigate uncharted territories. If you anchor yourself to the ground, acknowledge your fault in doing so instead of becoming frustrated in your inability to float toward the sky while watching others pass you by in your career and in life.

Another suggestion for how to confidently choose the sports car trajectory would be to become comfortable with doing uncomfortable things. No one becomes extraordinary by consistently being ordinary. Whether it is public speaking, a new proactive law enforcement initiative, or simply establishing a rapport with someone opposite your norm, these are all gas-pedal-pressing ways to push yourself to limits not thought of as possible before. I subscribed my children to this same system. I literally make them introduce and interact with someone who looks nothing like them at every opportunity I can. I swear by the effectiveness of this approach compared to that of the traditional learning environment. Whenever I attempt something outside of the police-prescribed culture and safe zone, I laugh off the criticisms, when in the past, I would internalize them and allow them to press my personal brake pedal instead. The result of my emergency brake engagement at the slightest onset of outside criticism would inevitably be the closure of yet another year. Simultaneously, the same slogan of what I "should really do" rang in my head. The "should do's" can easily concrete themselves into years of a career, with no foreseeable completion, as the catalyst event will never be allowed to present itself if one is obsessed with the outside cynics.

Just as the passing of an exotic sports car turns heads, so will heads be turned at an officer who drives this career path. Some will have deniable admiration, some will cast out their insecurity laced with negativity, some will have envy, and some will, in turn, emulate. The emulation is by far the most prominent sign of achievement on behalf of the officer whose path is being followed.

THE FINAL LESSON ON PATHS:

So would you like the midnight black or cherry red model?

Choosing the sports car path will lead to outside noise as you drive the hell out of that machine with the top down with the music blasting. Never hesitate to share the secret to your path or fail to invite others to jump in, but don't allow the critique of that path to cause you to press your brake pedal and turn around. Keep the gas pedal to the floor and throw out the rearview mirror. Drive down roads without a GPS and see where it takes you. Don't have a plan for everything because not everything can be planned. Be intelligently adaptable to unplanned events. Be spontaneous, be flexible, be open, and allow yourself to be you. If you realize someone else (in the field or your personal life) is stuck at the gas pump, flirting with the idea of emulating your courage, put some fuel in their tank and get them going. Giving the thumbs up to the driver of another sexy car, as you admire what that driver is experiencing, as you know it all too well, adds fuel to your tank too.

CHAPTER 11

Glass half full or half empty

The finish line is in sight, the taste of the civilian world has nearly grazed the lips, while the thought of normalcy is becoming more and more of a reality, but something about it seems misaligned. The very thing officers often covet the most, their pension and afterlife, have now been carefully prepared and delicately presented on the dining table, yet suddenly the appetite may seem suppressed. Not that one doesn't eagerly await to receive that first proof of payment or the chance at not setting the alarm, but something is off. Still, the various types of exhaustion that have been tattooed in some of our minds or injected into some of our souls leave with it a sense of senselessness.

This unfortunate tendency is one of the primary reasons for the composition of this book. What the hell is the point of all that selfless service, years of dedication safeguarding others, volumes of vigilance, and shared sacrifices, to only then crawl across and barely be capable of breaking through the flimsy banner strategically placed at the finish line? I can help, if you can hear. When you hear, you heal, and this will be avoidable. When you're healed, you have the ability and wherewithal to heal others.

If one dared argue the legitimacy of a genuine effect of the profession's cynicism on the officer's psyche, no further proof would be needed than that of the well-known yet under-acknowledged retirement dichotomy. Outsiders would easily see what we inherit at the end of a career to be a ticket to paradise. A secured yearly income, regardless of economic market swings, which in some cases tallies a greater sum than an annual income for some still actively working in their prime years. Clearly, this is meant to present food for thought and not actuaries. Some extreme examples of reported pension defaults have been noted in the last decade, which would cause some to argue that the certain future is uncertain. The point to be made and internalized is that in a simple breakdown, any blind survey would suggest that an officer reaching the retirement and pension collection phase of their life should be filled with nothing but joy and eager anticipation for what is next to come.

So if the perfect illustration of the retired officer is one with a sunburnt face, sombrero covered head, holding an umbrella drink while having wrinkles from extended smiles, why is the complete opposite so abundant in reality? Depression and suicide rates skyrocket upon retirement approaching, we hit the job market like a starving wolf in search of prey, while swearing that we cannot afford a single day without a secondary income, divorce rates seem to uptick at the moment that marital bliss should be rediscovered, and we get slapped with the reality that many of the intimate relationships we thought were preserved have spoiled beyond repair. So how can the end of our career rainbows so often house pots of mold instead of gold? Enter the theory of the empty glass.

THE LESSON OF THE GLASS:

Clean up spill...aisle four!

During our active years, we routinely add substance to our glasses. On average, five/six to one in terms of negatives to positives continually fill our glasses through the experiences in the field, in our departments, and certainly those interconnected with the codependency and effects of our personal lives. The issue with these substances being poured into our glasses is not just the negative connotation to them, but our inability and, sometimes, lack of opportunity, to properly empty them and lower the level of the substance in that glass. Without ever draining the glass, either through nutritious consumption or deliberate pouring, the substances spillover. When the substances spillover, they make a mess. Some may be offended at the elementary explanation I have provided here as if it is dumbed down. Yet, I can assure you, at the very moment you read this passage, a fellow officer is spilling their glass onto someone's lap, perhaps even their own, while causing an avoidable mess.

Many influences in my life, some law enforcement and some not, have displayed their genuine grasp of this concept and offered me sound advice on effectively managing it. Living in the moment and savoring all of the blessings in our lives creates a craving for repeat pleasur-able experiences. These cravings create symbolic thirst and assist us in consuming and eventually excreting the harmful substances poured into our glasses in a serene setting with organic results. Police officers are prime examples of "plea-sure-seekers." Lord knows this characteristic may have landed a few of us in "timeout" over the years, yet we are horrific at "pleasure-realizers." When we have pleasing experiences, especially from the non-law enforcement world, we routinely fail to stop and smell those beautiful roses right beneath our nostrils. When you are viewing, not watching that funny movie, or pretending to listen to a child's vivid account of their day at school because you are still preoccupied about the issues of work, the glass continues to fill because you haven't consumed and excreted anything that was in it before. Best-selling author and acclaimed speaker Jon Gordon readily claims that human beings cannot be grateful, pleasured, belly-laughing, and stressed/anxious at the same time. Consumption of one can certainly deplete the other. Pour it out.

One of the most productive ways to balance substance in a glass is to formulate and covet healthy relationships while protecting them with emotional overwatch. While shifts or tours have starts and ends, healthy relationships should not. When appropriately preserved in your active years, these relationships, forged in trust, love, and respect, can carry you through the uncertainty of the afterlife with security, passion, vigor, and vibrancy. On the contrary, these relationships are often neglected during the active years. It leaves us with a sense of embarrassment, regret, and self-pity, which often manifests itself in outward displays of aggression and resentment, as would be the case of an abused shelter pet. The soul and compassionate side are still somewhere in there. Yet, the years of mistrust, abuse, and deflection of feelings have created this hardened shell (the egg referenced earlier), which causes that shelter pet to instinctively lunge instead of habitually love. Many have asked me why do police officers neglect their familial relationships so frequently when they seem to be such prominent ambassadors of compassion and care for others, to which I have consistently responded with the mere fact that they (officers' families) are the most stable pieces to their lives. What one views as stable can simultaneously serve as one's preferred mechanism for neglect. I can go to my son's "next" game. My anniversary comes every year, so "next" year I'll make it memorable. It's my job, "they" get it.

I have personally spilled more family and or friend substances that I should have enjoyably consumed at the moment than I care to admit, and they are forever missed opportunities. And I can candidly admit that I did so because of the misguided sense of overconfidence I possessed in that I am such a prominent figure in their lives that they will undoubtedly give me a pass. This is a problematic aspect of our lives to admit as it is ugly, nasty, selfish, and the furthest from being what an officer should be; honorable. It is also the single fastest way to see toward the end of your career with that glass in rough shape, as your dominant hand shakes uncontrollably as you grasp it while trying to sip.

Even though our profession offers us the best variety

show the world has to offer, we tend to be creatures of methodical behaviors, which fit neatly within a squared life. By never taking chances or choosing non-traditional means, we also miss viable opportunities to fill our glasses with the "good things." I'm not suggesting sky-diving with a plastic bag. From being in the buffet line at the wedding and choosing something you've never eaten over the bland pasta, to being the first to try out a new piece of equipment issued to your department; being in a position to say, "I tried that and did/didn't like it," is so much more fulfilling than that of, "Hey, how was that, I've never tried it." The result of this ideology was proven to me on many occasions, but one, in particular, stands out.

I met a gentleman, "John," who just retired from a municipal police department a few years prior to our paths crossing. As John would explain, he had an average career at best but was grateful for the memories, the positive interactions he had, and the fact that he made it to retirement "generally" healthy. I couldn't help but notice the exquisite car he drove, and upon my envious compliment, John smirkingly chalked it up to being his "daily driver." John explained that he has experienced wealth beyond what he could have ever imagined but that the material things he has acquired pale in comparison to the experiences he now shares with his friends and family. Seeing my face flushed with confusion, as John could tell my intuitive retirement calculator was screaming errors, he explained that he was blessed with an opportunity simply because he asked.

John explained that as his career was starting to wind down, he retrospectively and regrettably found that he let his love for boating and the time spent with his son and friends doing so suffer. Whether it was due to an overtime shift, a late call, or a work-related function, he found himself routinely saying, "Next time," when he would be asked to visit the marina by those who loved him.

Until one Sunday morning, when he went to the marina, on his own accord, for a "just because," as we have all experienced at one time or another. While there, John became acquainted with a gentleman who owned a lovely vessel, as he specifically stated, who was in dire need of someone to serve as a guide as to overall boating safety, life-saving measures while onboard, security, and the like. This gentleman explained that he owned a fleet of yachts, which often chartered affluent trips throughout the world, for the most distinguished of clients, but that many of these same clients had no boating experience whatsoever which caused him tremendous anxiety. As they continued to converse, John told the gentleman about his career as an officer, but how much he admired someone who made a living on the seas as he has always been innately drawn to the water. As John was about to walk away, he decided to tell the gentleman that he'd be the perfect fit. With an impulse of audacity, John about-faced and approached the gentleman and confidently stated if he was looking for someone to fill that void, to look no further.

You see, John's attitude was similar to that of a no-lose situation, which provided him with all the confidence one could ever hope to muster. Needless to say, the offer came for John to fill the void. Certainly, his co-workers provided every reason why this couldn't possibly work out after he retires, because after all, that is what we are good at, with minimal effort. Officers routinely act as if they can see into the future, especially as to why things can't possibly work, all the while because we internally wish it could work for us. Today, John travels abroad while taking his son and friends on voyages they could have never imagined to some of the most remote destinations on the planet. His glass was refilled with all the delicious substance you could ask for!

Is everyone suited to ride yachts as trusted safety guides for their retirement gig and make exorbitant amounts of income? Probably not. The point herein is that if John didn't realize his glass was lacking the substances of what truly mattered in his life, he never would have mustered the courage to even ask the gentleman about the venture. John is a man that honorably completed a career as an officer and now, so deservingly, is enjoying the coolest retirement I've yet to encounter. John answered that question; why NOT me?

THE LAST GLASS LESSON:

Drinks are on the house!

You can fill your glass with the many wonders life has to offer as soon as you pass the first test of believing you are worthy to receive those blessings. Why shouldn't you get to enjoy the finer things? Why shouldn't you smile more than you frown, and instead of a dunce cap, wear the hell out of that crown? The active years in the profession will present many opportunities to add meaningful substances to your glass, so when the last page of the final chapter is read, you can sip from that same glass with poise, vitality, and grace. Seize these opportunities and never miss the equal amount of opportunities to pour out the sediment that falls to the bottom constructively. Pouring substance out and onto the floor only tends to leave a mess for someone else. Finding a trusted source as a drain for the overflow substance is a priceless person in your life, as they can comfort your fears of letting that substance go, along with the trauma accompanying it.

CONCLUSION

THE FINAL LESSON:

This ending is how we should all envision our ending; the ending should represent a closing that births an exciting new beginning. The best should always be yet to come, without ever neglecting and always embracing the current blessings while digesting our past experiences. Those experiences, both the positive and the negative, offer the opportunity to appreciate life for all it has to offer. With the proper mentality, the career path of law enforcement can undoubtedly be some of the most fulfilling years of your life. Immeasurable chances, challenges, and interactions will be presented where you can influence someone else's life path while always being mindful that your loved ones are along for the journey with you. Being selfless is at the cornerstone of a successful career, but that doesn't have to be interpreted as depriving yourself of the basic human dignity we should all be guaranteed. You cannot ever expect to get the best out of others until you are the best version of yourself. Allow yourself to fail, yet overcome. Allow yourself to stumble yet recover. Allow yourself to forgive and to be forgiven. Above all else, allow yourself to love and be loved.

This guide was built for the exact purpose a guide should be created; guidance. Nothing herein is meant to be followed without the insertion of individuality, creativity, and deviation to fit the personal goal path forward. Many of the perspectives provided are shared, yet rarely admitted, felt but rarely confessed, and unfortunately experienced when they can easily be avoided. The correctness tarp has been torn off the treasure chest of policing candor. We, the police, have committed ourselves to the endless pursuit of profession progression, have earnestly tried to address our deficiencies, have shown our ears to be noticeably larger than our mouths, and have endured society's expectation of not being allowed to fail. Bravery is throwing a vest over your shoulders each day, not having the slightest clue if it will just ache your back or save your life. Courage is genuinely displayed as a blend of the finest virtues, with the references in this book, as the men and women of law enforcement will continue forward on their path, acknowledge their shortcomings, and honorably serve selflessly.

I implore those in the field to use this guide as a mentorship and atlas. When success falls into your lap as you've uncovered the secret to that something, pay it forward, so another can enjoy the same sweetness. The only time to look down on anyone is to compliment their shoes. Follow the golden rule above all other rules. Be the coffee bean and transform your surroundings into seeing your collective goodness infect those around you.

I implore those not in the field to open their minds to understanding. The choice to open your heart is a personal one, and I respect that, but the choice to offer insight without a solidified pledge of agreement is a path to a better tomorrow for **all of us**. One-way streets are inefficient, cause traffic jams, and frustrate all who traverse them. We don't expect or believe that those not in the field should understand what it is like to be us, but only hope that those same will understand not to oppose us automatically.

Here's to being one.

Here's to being well.

- TR

ABOUT THE AUTHOR

Born into a blue-collar family, with ties to the New York City Police Department, Thomas Rizzo knew early on that his undeniable calling was to become a police officer. In the dusk of the infamous attacks on September 11, 2001, this calling became a reality within a small borough in central New Jersey.

With an insatiable curiosity to learn and broaden horizons, Rizzo transferred to a much larger agency and jurisdiction just a few years later. As his personal life progressed through marriage and children, so did his career.

As an avid learner of human behaviors and committed student of leadership philosophies, Rizzo rose through the police ranks and obtained graduate-level education in the academic environment.

As an Adjunct Professor for nearly ten years, Rizzo blended his police persona into that of a teacher within a classroom.

Believing in the human spirit, Rizzo has strongly advocated for the significance of transformational leader tendencies and the amazing power of perspective, in this latest work to help guide those on the path of a law enforcement career, officers' loved ones, and as a candid discussion piece for those opposed to the profession.

To learn more, visit www.ThomasRizzo.com.